Improving Learning
with Information Technology

Report of a Workshop

Steering Committee on Improving Learning
with Information Technology

Gail E. Pritchard, *Editor*

Center for Education

Division of Behavioral and Social Sciences and Education

National Research Council

NATIONAL ACADEMY PRESS
Washington, DC

NATIONAL ACADEMY PRESS   2101 Constitution Avenue, N.W.   Washington, DC 20418

NOTICE: The project that is the subject of this report was approved by the Governing Board of the National Research Council, whose members are drawn from the councils of the National Academy of Sciences, the National Academy of Engineering, and the Institute of Medicine. The members of the committee responsible for the report were chosen for their special competences and with regard for appropriate balance.

This study was supported by Contract/Grant No. R303U000001 between the National Academy of Sciences and the U.S. Department of Education. Any opinions, findings, conclusions, or recommendations expressed in this publication are those of the author(s) and do not necessarily reflect the views of the organizations or agencies that provided support for the project.

International Standard Book Number 0-309-08413-X

Additional copies of this report are available from National Academy Press, 2101 Constitution Avenue, N.W., Lockbox 285, Washington, DC 20055; (800) 624-6242 or (202) 334-3313 (in the Washington metropolitan area); Internet, http://www.nap.edu

Printed in the United States of America

Copyright 2002 by the National Academy of Sciences. All rights reserved.

Suggested citation: National Research Council. (2002). *Improving learning with information technology: Report of a workshop.* Steering Committee on Improving Learning with Information Technology. G.E. Pritchard (Ed.), Center for Education, Division of Behavioral and Social Sciences and Education. Washington, DC: National Academy Press.

THE NATIONAL ACADEMIES

National Academy of Sciences
National Academy of Engineering
Institute of Medicine
National Research Council

The **National Academy of Sciences** is a private, nonprofit, self-perpetuating society of distinguished scholars engaged in scientific and engineering research, dedicated to the furtherance of science and technology and to their use for the general welfare. Upon the authority of the charter granted to it by the Congress in 1863, the Academy has a mandate that requires it to advise the federal government on scientific and technical matters. Dr. Bruce M. Alberts is president of the National Academy of Sciences.

The **National Academy of Engineering** was established in 1964, under the charter of the National Academy of Sciences, as a parallel organization of outstanding engineers. It is autonomous in its administration and in the selection of its members, sharing with the National Academy of Sciences the responsibility for advising the federal government. The National Academy of Engineering also sponsors engineering programs aimed at meeting national needs, encourages education and research, and recognizes the superior achievements of engineers. Dr. Wm. A. Wulf is president of the National Academy of Engineering.

The **Institute of Medicine** was established in 1970 by the National Academy of Sciences to secure the services of eminent members of appropriate professions in the examination of policy matters pertaining to the health of the public. The Institute acts under the responsibility given to the National Academy of Sciences by its congressional charter to be an adviser to the federal government and, upon its own initiative, to identify issues of medical care, research, and education. Dr. Kenneth I. Shine is president of the Institute of Medicine.

The **National Research Council** was organized by the National Academy of Sciences in 1916 to associate the broad community of science and technology with the Academy's purposes of furthering knowledge and advising the federal government. Functioning in accordance with general policies determined by the Academy, the Council has become the principal operating agency of both the National Academy of Sciences and the National Academy of Engineering in providing services to the government, the public, and the scientific and engineering communities. The Council is administered jointly by both Academies and the Institute of Medicine. Dr. Bruce M. Alberts and Dr. Wm. A. Wulf are chairman and vice chairman, respectively, of the National Research Council.

**STEERING COMMITTEE
ON IMPROVING LEARNING WITH
INFORMATION TECHNOLOGY**

ROY PEA *(Cochair),* Stanford University, Palo Alto, CA
WM. A. WULF *(Cochair),* National Academy of Engineering, Washington, DC
MIRIAM MASULLO, IBM Thomas J. Watson Research Center, Yorktown Heights, NY
JAMES W. PELLEGRINO, University of Illinois at Chicago
LOU PUGLIESE, Consultant, Herndon, VA

KEVIN AYLESWORTH, *Study Director*
SUSAN GOLDMAN, *Special Consultant,* University of Illinois at Chicago
JAY LABOV, *Deputy Director*
GAIL E. PRITCHARD, *Program Officer*
TINA WINTERS, *Research Assistant*
TERRY HOLMER, *Senior Project Assistant*
DOUG SPRUNGER, *Senior Project Assistant*

COMMITTEE ON IMPROVING LEARNING WITH INFORMATION TECHNOLOGY

ROY PEA *(Cochair),* Stanford University, Palo Alto, CA
WM. A. WULF *(Cochair),* National Academy of Engineering, Washington, DC
BARBARA ALLEN, Project LemonLINK, Lemon Grove, CA
EDWARD R. DIETERLE II, Northwestern High School, Mitchellville, MD
DAVID DWYER, Apple Computer, Inc., Palo Alto, CA
LOUIS GOMEZ, Northwestern University, Evanston, IL
AMY JO KIM, NAIMA, El Granada, CA
EDWARD D. LAZOWSKA, University of Washington, Seattle, WA
MIRIAM MASULLO, IBM Thomas J. Watson Research Center, Yorktown Heights, NY
JAMES W. PELLEGRINO, University of Illinois at Chicago
LOU PUGLIESE, Consultant, Herndon, VA
MARSHALL S. SMITH, William and Flora Hewlett Foundation, Menlo Park, CA
BOB TINKER, Concord Consortium, Concord, MA
DAVID VOGT, Brainium.com, Vancouver, BC, Canada
BARBARA WATKINS, Chicago Public Schools
LINDA WILSON, International SEMATECH, Austin, TX

KEVIN AYLESWORTH, *Study Director*
SUSAN GOLDMAN, *Special Consultant*, University of Illinois at Chicago
HERB S. LIN, *Senior Scientist*, Division on Engineering and Physical Sciences
TIMOTHY READY, *Senior Program Officer,* Board on Behavioral, Cognitive, and Sensory Sciences and Education
GAIL E. PRITCHARD, *Program Officer*
TINA WINTERS, *Research Assistant*
TERRY HOLMER, *Senior Project Assistant*
DOUG SPRUNGER, *Senior Project Assistant*

Acknowledgments

The ILIT steering committee would like to thank the many symposium participants listed in Appendix A. The frank and vigorous discussions contributed greatly to the subsequent deliberations of the ILIT committee. The committee welcomes these participants to its larger community of interested parties and invites them and others to "continue the conversation" by participating on the ILIT website, <http://www.nrcilit.org>.

The committee would also like to commend the representatives of successful partnership projects engaging these three communities who attended the meeting and shared the histories of their programs. Barbara Allen and Darryl LaGace shared their insight in developing and managing Project LemonLINK, based in Lemon Grove, California, which focuses on high-speed connectivity; equitable, adequate access to resources; development of web-based instructional tools; and ongoing professional development for teachers. Fred Carrigg and students Steven Perez and José Marrero talked about the transformation of the Union City, New Jersey, public schools from a failing system to a national exemplar. The Chicago City Science program was presented by Barbara Watkins, then principal of James McCosh Elementary School (now chief education officer of the Chicago public schools); Irene DaMota, principal of Roberto Clemente High School; and Louis Gomez, associate professor at Northwestern University. James Kaput of the University of Massachusetts, Dartmouth, explained the goals of the SimCalc project, which aims to introduce powerful mathematical ideas early by using techniques that tap into children's natural abilities.

Finally, the evening of January 24, 2001, John Bransford, Vanderbilt University, and Nora Sabelli, University of Texas at Austin, provided overviews of the report *How People Learn* and K-12 education issues, respectively, as context for subsequent symposium work.

Within the NRC, the committee would like to thank Kevin Aylesworth, senior program officer and study director in the Center for Education (CFE), for his able guidance as study director of this project, and Jay Labov, deputy director of the CFE, for his general oversight. Susan Goldman, now at the University of Illinois at Chicago but originally at Vanderbilt University's Learning Technology Center, is a special consultant to the project and has provided counsel and suggestions on many of its facets. Herb Lin, senior scientist at the Computer Science and Telecommunications Board, Division on Engineering and Physical Sciences, and Timothy Ready and Suzanne Donovan, senior program officers in the Division of Behavioral and Social Sciences and Education, provided additional guidance and perspective from their respective communities. The steering committee extends its deep appreciation to David Sibbet, president of the Grove Consultants International, for his talented and creative moderating of many of the symposium sessions. Thanks are also due Terry Holmer, CFE senior project assistant, for her capable logistical coordination of the workshop and committee meetings. Doug Sprunger, CFE senior project assistant, has the considerable task of creating and maintaining the ILIT committee's online presence, including its website and discussion log. Tina Winters, CFE research assistant, has been instrumental in identifying and organizing research for the project. Finally, Gail Pritchard, CFE program officer, has had the chief responsibility of distilling the rich discussions of the workshop into this summary report, which will be used to launch future discussions with other colleagues interested in improving American education with information technology.

This report has been reviewed in draft form by individuals chosen for their diverse perspectives and technical expertise, in accordance with procedures approved by the NRC's Report Review Committee. The purpose of this independent review is to provide candid and critical comments that will assist the National Academies in making the published report as sound as possible and to ensure that the report meets institutional standards for objectivity, evidence, and responsiveness to the study charge. The review comments and draft manuscript remain confidential to protect the integrity of the deliberative process. We wish to thank the following individuals for their review of this report: *Carol E. Edwards*, National Foundation for the Improvement of Education, Washington, DC; *Janet L. Kolodner*, Georgia Institute of Technology; *Ronald M. Latanision*, Massachusetts Institute of Technology; *James W. Serum*, Viaken Systems, Inc., Gaithersburg, MD; and *Gary Smith*, Montgomery County Public Schools, MD.

Although the reviewers listed above have provided many constructive comments and suggestions, they were not asked to endorse the final draft of the report before its release. The review of this report was overseen by Scott Stowell, Spokane Public Schools. Appointed by the National Research Council, he was responsible for ensuring that an independent examination of this report was carried out in accordance with institutional procedures and that all review comments were carefully considered. Responsibility for the final content of this report rests entirely with the authoring committee and the institution.

Roy Pea and Wm. A. Wulf, *Cochairs*
Committee on Improving Learning with Information Technology

Contents

PREFACE — xiii

INTRODUCTION: TRANSFORMING K-12
EDUCATION WITH INFORMATION TECHNOLOGY — 1

1   INITIAL ILIT ACTIVITY: A SYMPOSIUM — 3
    Timing Is Everything, 3
    Committee Goals, 8
    Evening Sessions, 11
    Opening Comments: Participant Observations Concerning
    Obstacles and Challenges, 14
    Exemplars: It Can Be Done, 21

2   SYMPOSIUM ACTIVITY: FORGING A
    COMMON LANGUAGE, BUILDING ALLIANCES — 29
    Activity Background and Scope, 29

3   CONTINUING THE CONVERSATION — 47
    The ILIT Committee's Charge to the Nation, 47
    Next Steps, 48
    Solicitations and Requests, 53

REFERENCES — 55

APPENDIX A: SYMPOSIUM PARTICIPANT LIST — 59

APPENDIX B: SYMPOSIUM AGENDA — 65

Preface

Throughout the 1990s, the United States enjoyed the longest peacetime expansion of its economy in history, fueled in large measure by innovation in information technology (IT) and the expanded applications of IT into other sectors of society. However, most of these technologies—and the genius, creativity, and financial and intellectual capital that have undergirded them—have focused nearly exclusively on industrial needs and applications and the entertainment sector, while specific applications for the educational realm have been largely neglected.[1] Even so, fueled substantially by E-rate funding,[2] public schools in the United States spent

---

[1] See President's Committee of Advisors on Science and Technology, 1997, and President's Information Technology Advisory Committee, 1999.

[2] The Schools and Libraries Program—often called the "E-rate"—provides support for eligible schools and libraries to help offset the cost of advanced telecommunications services. Since its inception, the E-rate program has provided about $2 billion to schools and libraries. Eligible schools and libraries receive discounts ranging from 20 to 90 percent on telecommunications services, including local and long-distance service, Internet access, and internal connection projects such as wiring and networking schools and libraries to facilitate the use of advanced telecommunications technology. The amount of discount available to a school or library is determined by the income level of students in the community and whether the location is urban or rural. Income level for a school or district is measured by the percentage of students eligible for the National School Lunch Program (NSLP), administered by the U.S. Department of Agriculture. Applicants for E-rate assistance must develop an approved "technology plan" explaining how acquiring advanced technologies or discounts on existing technologies will help them in their day-to-day operations or in fulfilling the goals of their organizations. For more information, see <http://www.sl.universalservice.org>.

nearly $6 billion on technology during the 1999-2000 school year alone (Carvin, 2000).

In spring 2000, representatives from the U.S. Department of Education (DOEd) and senior staff at the National Research Council (NRC) recognized a common frustration: that the potential of information technology to transform K-12 education remains unrealized. School-initiated efforts to improve teaching and learning through the use of IT have largely been devoid of input from cognitive sciences[3] research, which has elucidated modern principles of human learning and their implications for improving education (e.g., the NRC's 1999 report, *How People Learn*). Meanwhile, computing power is increasing while costs are significantly decreasing. This combination—knowing more about how people learn, combined with a continuing trajectory of greater computing power at a much lower price—provides the essential elements to tackling the challenge of creating effective information technologies for educational purposes. In fall 2000 the U.S. DOEd formally requested that the National Academies undertake an interdisciplinary project called Improving Learning with Information Technology (ILIT) to meld expertise among practitioners in the chief domains:

- experts in the cognitive and learning sciences who have explored the practical uses of IT in education;
- practitioners in the education community who understand the opportunities and the challenges for the ways in which educators can most effectively organize their working lives and carry out their many tasks, particularly in the face of changing demands for knowledge creating and handling skills in the new economy (Marshall and Tucker, 1992), and
- hardware, software, and applications developers who are committed to improving education. The hardware sector can adapt its commercial equipment to better meet the organizational, financial, and technological constraints of the K-12 community. Software and applications developers can develop new tools or new applications for existing tools that can be used productively in the education domain.

---

[3]Throughout this report, the terms "learning sciences" and "cognitive sciences" are used interchangeably to refer to the body of knowledge about how people learn.

For the first phase, the following three goals were identified:[4]

1. to establish ongoing dialogue and interactions among the technology, learning and cognition, and education practitioner communities for the purpose of improving education for all learners through the development and appropriate uses of modern technology;
2. to find ways to incorporate the knowledge base, research findings, and innovations from each of these communities into coherent strategic approaches to developing education technologies; and
3. to offer information so that the end users of education technologies can make better informed decisions about the purchase, use, and maintenance of these technologies and, in addition, can develop the capacity to offer the kinds of professional development programs that will enable teachers to use education technologies in ways that can transform teaching and learning.

Wm. A. Wulf, president of the National Academy of Engineering and professor of computer science at the University of Virginia, and Roy Pea, professor of education at Stanford University (and formerly of SRI International), agreed to serve as cochairs of the project. Following the appointment of a small steering committee, the project was launched with a symposium on January 24-25, 2001 (see Appendix A for the participant list and Appendix B for the symposium agenda). Subsequent to the symposium, the second phase of the project included appointing a full committee to undertake continued deliberations on this issue. The committee is composed of 16 people who are leading experts in the fields of cognition and learning, education practice, information technology, community building, and technology roadmapping. The committee will have several deliberative meetings, solicit the input of other experts, and host additional workshops and meetings to draw local and regional issues into the national picture. In addition to this report of the opening symposium, the committee will produce a final report (anticipated to be available in December 2002). The second major activity of the committee was a work-

---

[4]Because of the interdisciplinary nature of this project, it was organized and implemented collaboratively by the National Research Council's Center for Education, Division of Behavioral and Social Sciences and Education, and the Computer Science and Telecommunications Board, Division on Engineering and Physical Sciences.

shop in December 2001 to further the community-building process and to begin roadmapping the issue. The final activity of the committee will be a major symposium in fall 2002; this symposium will bring the community together again for the purpose of building a standing body of experts to monitor learning with information technology and to plan future activities as appropriate. In addition to the reports to be produced, another committee product will be an interactive website to promote the growth of the community.

This report summarizes the proceedings of the symposium and is intended for people interested in considering better strategies for using information technology in the educational arena. While it offers insights from the presenters on both the challenges to and the opportunities for forging a better dialogue among learning scientists, technologists, and educators, it does not contain conclusions or recommendations. Rather, it highlights issues to consider, constituents to engage, and strategies to employ in the effort to build a coalition to harness the power of information technologies for the improvement of American education. Every effort has been made to convey the speakers' content and viewpoints accurately. Recognizing the speculative nature of many of the speaker contributions, most attributions identify a speaker by area of expertise rather than by name. The report reflects the proceedings of the workshop and is not intended to be a comprehensive review of all the issues involved in the project to improve learning with information technology.

Introduction

Transforming K-12 Education with Information Technology

Handheld computers or personal digital assistants (PDAs) were launched in the marketplace in 1996. Within 18 months, these handheld devices had swept through the business community and virtually transformed the way people took notes and kept professional and personal calendars. Today, PDAs can connect to the Internet and provide a variety of services, from scouting out restaurants in the vicinity to using the global positioning system (GPS) and enabling enterprise-wide knowledge management systems. This is but one example of the power of technology on a grand scale, transforming how people work and play.

Why hasn't technology, be it hardware or software, had the same transformative effect on K-12 education? The National Research Council's (NRC) project on Improving Learning with Information Technology (ILIT) was created to confront this question and ultimately to enable the transformation of K-12 education through information technology. It will accomplish these goals by bringing together representatives of the K-12 education, IT industry, and learning sciences communities to roadmap the improvement of K-12 education through information technology.

The initial activity of this project was a symposium that was held on January 24-25, 2001. This publication is a report of the events that took place at the symposium.

1

Initial ILIT Activity: A Symposium

TIMING IS EVERYTHING

On January 24, 2001, Dr. Wm. A. Wulf, president of the National Academy of Engineering and cochair of the steering committee on Improving Learning with Information Technology (ILIT), opened the symposium by outlining the confluence of issues and opportunities that catalyzed the project:

- **National Will**—The Bush administration's first legislative act was to issue his education plan, *No Child Left Behind*. Wulf believed that both the emphasis of the proposed legislation and its timing reflected a growing national recognition of the need to address the problems of K-12 education in America.
- **How People Learn**—The cognitive and social science advances explicated in *How People Learn* (National Research Council (NRC), 1999b) have provided the academic and research communities with a more precise, scientifically based understanding of how people construct personal knowledge and understanding from infancy to adulthood.
- **Computing Power**—In the past decade, information technology has become relatively inexpensive, very powerful, and nearly ubiquitous.[1]

---

[1] How to increase access to education technologies and minimize the digital divide—defined broadly as socioeconomic disparities in access to information technology—were important themes of this workshop and of the ILIT project itself. Additional discussions on these topics can be found later in this text. Also see Pea, 2001.

These vital elements position policy makers, cognitive researchers, teachers and administrators, and technologists to work together effectively to harness the power of information technology so that it can transform the productivity of K-12 education, just as it has done for the business community and many other aspects of society.

Cochair Roy Pea followed Wulf. He began his remarks by quoting John Chambers, CEO of Cisco Systems: "The next big killer application for the Internet is going to be education." (Friedman, 1999). Pea thought this comment indicated that the time was ripe for the ILIT project. He identified the following "megatrends" within the educational landscape that could aid the project by coalescing the three principal communities:

- **Learning Sciences Research**—*How People Learn* (NRC, 1999b) explains the solid scientific basis for guiding advances in curriculum, pedagogy, teacher education, and assessment. A corollary project on bridging theory and practice (NRC, 1999c) discusses the divide between what is known in the learning sciences and what appears in teacher education programs, reform agendas, textbook and technology-based curricula, and the public perception. *How People Learn: Bridging Research and Practice* provides powerful insights and paradigms for using technology to support learning, such as incorporating authentic and engaging inquiry-based tasks, drawing upon real-world contexts for learning, connecting experts and communities of learners, and considering the social aspects of computing. New approaches to visualization and analysis make very complicated subjects much more accessible through animation, visualization, and other techniques that tap the multiple intelligences of different learners and sustain new forms of learning conversations. Computing can enable complex problem solving that lets students do more challenging things than they could do without it by "scaffolding" their activities. Information technology facilitates opportunities for feedback, reflection, and revision through paradigms ranging from intelligent tutoring systems to more complicated ones that provide frequent assessment and context to guide instruction. IT also permits more focused attention on teacher learning in online communities of practice and other paradigms. While teachers are unlikely to be replaced by these technologies, IT creates new and interesting opportunities and challenges to the ways in which educators can most effectively organize their working lives and carry out their many tasks as lifelong learners and professionals.

- **Standards and Accountability**—Pea credited the work of the state governors and organizations such as the National Council of Teachers of Mathematics, the American Association for the Advancement of Science, and the National Academies for developing mathematics and science standards that have contributed to the nationwide effort to achieve excellence in education. Coupled with these standards is a greater emphasis on proof that students are achieving the educational goals.[2]
- **K-12 Technology Infrastructure and the Impact of the E-Rate**[3]—The K-12 technology infrastructure has been rapidly changing through the investment of close to $6 billion in the E-rate and other state and industry funds, so that now there is an infrastructure upon which to build. This means that almost all public schools and three-quarters of instructional rooms are connected to the Internet (Cattagni and Ferris, 2001), although wide socioeconomic disparities still persist (National Telecommunications and Information Administration, 2000). Furthermore, 70 percent of the nation's K-12 teachers also have PCs and Internet connections at home, which affords another avenue to reach and influence them.
- **Technology Purchasing Challenge**—Pea highlighted some particular challenges within the school administrative infrastructure regarding the acquisition of technology. He believes that those who purchase technology for schools are hamstrung because they have difficulty in finding out what products are readily available and appropriate for their needs. Furthermore, he noted that those who are likely to use the technologies in schools—primarily teachers and students—are rarely the ones who buy the products or influence the buying decisions. Instead, that responsibility tends to fall on administrators and parents, who may be swayed by considerations other than the educational effectiveness of the products.
- **Teaching Workforce**—Linked to other changes taking place in the K-12 environment is a wave of changes in the teacher workforce. Accord-

---

[2]While there was some discussion of the danger of overtesting and test preparation dominating the school day, the discussion centered on the national desire for more concrete accountability of student performance. For more information on the ramifications of overtesting, see NRC, 1998.

[3]The timing of the symposium coincided with the change in administration and several participants expressed concern about whether the new administration would continue the same level of support for educational services such as the E-rate and distance education initiatives as the previous administration. In fact, while the symposium was taking place, President Bush placed a hold on all E-rate funds.

ing to figures provided by the National Center for Education Statistics (Hussar, 1999) and others, nearly two million new teachers will need to enter the workforce by 2008 to replace those who will be retiring or leaving the profession for other reasons. Colleges and universities are not likely to educate enough new teachers to meet the classroom staffing needs of the schools. This means that many new teachers are likely to be uncertified or at least less qualified than they need to be (see Olson, 2000), especially given the increasing demands for academic excellence and accountability in the nation's public schools.

Professional development issues for current teachers also pose significant challenges (see for example, (NRC, 1996b, 2000; National Commission on Mathematics and Science Teaching for the 21st Century, 2000). In U.S. high schools, a third of the teachers of mathematics, a quarter of those in English, and a fifth in science are teaching without a college major or minor in the fields in which they are teaching. As data have shown, deep knowledge of the content and processes of a discipline is critically important to successful teaching (Darling-Hammond, 1996, 1997; Stodolsky, 1988). Pedagogy alone cannot equip a teacher to teach effectively.

- **Attention to Improving Education from Policy Makers and the Business Community**—The policy makers and business community have paid extraordinary attention to improving education in recent years. The CEO Forum on Education and Technology[4] and other groups continually identify education, readiness of the workforce, and related issues as their first priority in addressing critical issues (see for example, NRC, 1999a, 2001).

- **K-12 Education as a Driving Market Influence**—There is a perception among the investment community that K-12 education is a major underdeveloped marketplace. Merrill Lynch, which has funded several feasibility studies in this area, says that the $360 billion K-12 sector is the largest in the cradle-to-grave education industry, but the most difficult in which to invest (Moe et al., 2000). Companies that provide materials to

---

[4]The CEO Forum on Education and Technology was founded in fall 1996 to help ensure that America's schools effectively prepare all students to be contributing citizens and productive workers in the 21st century. To meet this objective, the Forum plans to issue an annual assessment of the nation's progress toward integrating technology into American classrooms through the year 2000. For more information, see <http://www.ceoforum.org/>.

public education must deal with fragmented school markets; different local and state policies for developing and adopting curricula, textbooks, and other materials for use in the schools; and long adoption cycles. Despite the huge size of K-12 education market, there is a general perception that because of its exceptional fragmentation the education marketplace simply does not function as other sectors of the economy (Web-Based Education Commission, 2000).

- **The Power and Ubiquity of Computing**—Moore's Law predicts that the power of the microprocessor will double every 12 to 18 months (Webopedia, available at http://www.webopedia.com). Metcalfe's Law says that the potential value of a network is the square of the number of nodes connected to the network, whether the network consists of phones or computers (Gilder, 1993). Today, modern information technology is becoming ever more powerful and efficient and doing so in less time than predicted by Moore's Law. Developments in technology are resulting in greater and greater miniaturization, portability, digital convergence, and increased bandwidth even as costs are falling. Recent advances include applications-based networking, the application service provider (ASP) model, different platforms such as handhelds, thin client servers, peer-to-peer and wireless networks, and digital cameras, videocams, and MP3 music players.

One of the most interesting outcomes of these developments has been a sustainable marketplace for e-learning in the past couple of years. Although at present most e-learning services are connected to universities rather than K-12 education, that could change.

- **The Changing Workforce**[5]—Quality education is an imperative for an information-driven economy and society. The kinds of analytical skills that information technology begins to bring into work and the knowledge economy create new demands on education. As the modern workplace becomes increasingly complex, workers face new intellectual demands—and indeed, with biogenetic and other scientific breakthroughs, the country needs a better-informed citizenry. Pea urged participants to keep in mind that today's students will be most directly affected by and come to lead in facing the challenges posed by these rapid global transformations. The leaders of tomorrow are in school today, and it is incumbent on the educational system to help them learn in ways that will improve their future and the future of society.

---

[5]See NRC, 1999a.

- **The Fourth Wave of the Internet**—Technological advancement began with the fundamental net protocols developed by the Defense Advanced Research Projects Agency (DARPA) and government agency contractor work; it then evolved into bulletin boards and online services; this was followed by the web with its capability for rich text, graphics, and images. The emerging fourth wave, as characterized by Norman Winarsky (Sarnoff Labs, 2000), is expected to bring four major dimensions of explosive growth:

- ubiquitous connectivity, starting with the connected PC;
- media richness, which began with text, evolved to text and graphics, and continues with the creation of audio and video capability and 3D interactive, immersive worlds;
- IT capacity, moving toward much faster processing, nearly unlimited storage, and much faster bandwidth connectivity;
- increasingly smarter services, from simple browsers to search engines capable of personalized and customized search.

Box 1.1 below provides a sampling of data to indicate the advancements on the horizon. The alignment of these crucial elements—a deeper understanding of how people learn, coupled with robust computer power available at cheaper cost—appears to indicate tremendous potential for affordable, personal portable gateways to e-learning, which will eventually become available to all students and teachers. Current research in the cognitive sciences coupled with the power of emerging IT should make it possible to provide fundamentally better real-time teaching and assessment capabilities in classrooms. Ready access to IT specifically designed for improving education should provide opportunities for meaningful, career-enhancing professional development for many more teachers in the myriad settings that constitute today's and tomorrow's education environments. Access to this kind of quality professional development would enable teachers to learn about advances in education research and about the kinds of tools that are available to support their efforts both in and outside of the classroom.

COMMITTEE GOALS

The project sponsor, the U.S. Department of Education, and the committee of the ILIT project recognize that these opportunities for improving

Box 1.1
Information Technology Horizon

- 12/2002   Digital Music/rap/talk-radio expected to hit inflection point in units sold per year
- 1/2003 $600 PC with MPEG-4 decode & encode expected to be in 80 percent of machines in use in homes
- 6/2003   Third-generation Visual MUD (Multiuser Domains) and MOOs (Object-Oriented Multiuser Domains)
- 12/2003   60 percent of children age 7 to 18 expected to have Internet-enhanced cell phones, pagers, PDAs
- 12/2003   95 percent of homes with children expected to have Internet access (through cable, Playstation, iPhone, etc.)
- 12/2003   Active advertising expected to be in more than 5,000 elevators and at bus stops
- 1/2004   E-mail inboxes that automatically reject e-mail from those not on the recipient's list are expected to exceed one million
- 2004   89 million information appliances (excluding cell phones) expected to ship each year
- 6/2004   Homes with cable modem and DSL deployment projected to exceed 35 million
- 12/2004   Video cell phones affordable in urban areas in the U.S. (from third-generation wireless providers)
- 12/2005   HDTV-ready TVs and converter boxes expected to sell at the rate of 15 million/year

SOURCE: Adapted from data compiled from Forrester Research, Jupiter Media Metrix, and IDC.[6]

---

[6]Forrester Research is an independent research firm that analyzes the future of technology change and its impact on businesses, consumers, and society; Jupiter Media Metrix delivers analysis, measurement, advice, and events to provide businesses with global resources for understanding and profiting from the Internet; IDC is a provider of technology intelligence, industry analysis, market data, and strategic and tactical guidance to builders, providers, and users of information technology.

education cannot be viewed only as promises for the future. There are difficult challenges to bringing the full potential of IT to bear on improving teaching and learning. The creation of cutting-edge technology designed for specific educational goals and needs will require coordination and cooperation by the best thinkers and planners in information technology, the sciences of learning, and the educational community. New and evolving knowledge, strategies, and mechanisms will be required to meet the current and future needs of schools and other educational settings.

Over the timeline for this project, the committee expects to establish ongoing dialogue and interactions among the three sectors—the IT industry, the learning sciences, and the education community. The committee will need to find ways to tap the knowledge, research, and innovations of each of these communities, because they all must become fundamental contributors to the process of improving teaching and learning. Strategies must be developed to allow the end users of the technology to make more strategic and informed decisions about what hardware and software to purchase, how to maintain it, and how to best employ it to transform teaching and learning. Professional development and ongoing institutional support will be required to prepare teachers to use the technology most effectively. At the same time, decisions by end users need to be made with the understanding that the IT industry has recognized and responded to the true needs of education consumers, and that it has designed its products in accordance with what is known about human learning, as well as the current realities and future opportunities of the K-12 education system.

Pea acknowledged that the different constituencies who were invited to this symposium and who will contribute to the remainder of the project have diverse goals, different criteria for success, and different perceptions of the constraints that block that success. There are friction points among these communities that must be addressed forthrightly. He urged participants to move beyond current barriers and obstacles to establish mutual respect, recognition, and trust, because everyone has something to bring to the table. How can these communities be energized to work together in powerful new ways, to richly envision the future of learning technology? This is the greatest challenge. If it can be accomplished, it will provide the most promising route to serving the needs of the education community.

Finally, Pea said that the ILIT committee wants to find pathways to partnerships that will leverage the collective intelligence of the three communities. To do this, the committee's first goal will be to build a common language that will lead to an understanding of the priorities and perspectives of each of the communities. To this end, part of this symposium and the future activities of the committee will include analyzing and reflecting on case studies of partnership projects and examining processes, outcomes, and products of those efforts. Symposium participants will need to ask tough questions about why a particular strategy or approach worked or did not work, how challenges were overcome, and which strategies for success could be used in other settings.

Linda Roberts, former director of the Office of Educational Technology at the U.S. Department of Education at the time of the symposium, concluded the welcoming remarks by briefly sharing wisdom garnered from her lengthy experience at the intersection between education and IT. She recommended the following: having a vision, staying focused, recognizing the incentives and using them, and, finally, providing a common vocabulary. She concluded by urging participants not only to really think about the future, but "to do the future."

EVENING SESSIONS

Following the first day's activities, two guest speakers shared their expertise on two crucial topics for the project to improve learning with information technology. First, John Bransford, chair of the committee that produced *How People Learn: Brain, Mind, Experience, and School* (HPL), published by NRC in 1999, offered a short presentation on how children learn and the influence and impact of technology on learning.

Bransford reported that the HPL committee concluded that learning is a basic, adaptive function of humans. People are designed to be flexible learners and active agents in acquiring knowledge and skills. While acknowledging that people learn many things without formal instruction, the committee found that formal training is usually necessary to learn reading, mathematics, the sciences, literature, and the history of a society, and the school is the traditional venue for this learning. Bransford said that learning in science, mathematics, and history has become more challenging because of their growing volume of information and increasing complexity. On the other hand, recent research provides a deep understanding of complex reasoning and performance on problem-solving tasks and how skill and understanding are acquired.

In the last 30 years, research has generated new conceptions of learning in five areas, which Bransford highlighted for the participants:

- **Memory and Structure of Knowledge**—Knowing how learners develop coherent structures of information has been particularly useful in understanding the nature of organized knowledge that underlies effective comprehension and thinking.
- **Analysis of Problem Solving and Reasoning**—New research on expert learners has enabled learning theory to account for how learners acquire skills to search a problem space and then use these general strategies in many problem-solving situations. The result has been a clear distinction between problem-solving skills in novice learners and the specialized expertise of individuals who have proficiency in particular subjects.
- **Early Foundations**—Scientific studies of infants and young children have revealed the relationships between children's learning predispositions and their emergent abilities to organize and coordinate information, make inferences, and discover strategies for problem solving.
- **Metacognitive Processes and Self-Regulatory Capabilities**—Individuals can be taught to regulate their behaviors, and these regulatory activities enable self-monitoring and executive control of one's performance.
- **Cultural Experience and Community Participation**—Learning is promoted by social norms that value the search for understanding. Early learning is assisted by the supportive context of the family and the social environment, and through the kinds of activities in which adults do with children.

Bransford also shared the committee's findings regarding new information technologies. He said that a number of the features of new technologies appear to be consistent with the principles of a new science of learning. For instance, new technologies that afford increased interactivity have the potential to create more environments for students to learn by doing, to receive regular feedback for improvement, and to refine their understanding and development of new knowledge. Students can use visualization and modeling software tools to increase their conceptual understanding. New technologies provide access to a vast array of information, including digital libraries, real-world data to use in analyses, and linkage to remote experts and others who can provide information, feedback, and inspiration, all of which can enhance the learning of teachers and administrators as well as students. Bransford commented that there are many ways that technology can be used to help create such environments, both for teachers and for students. However, he also noted that many issues arise in considering how to educate teachers to use new technologies effectively. For instance, what do teachers need to know about learning processes? About technology? What kinds of training are most effective for helping teachers use high-quality instructional programs? What is the best way to use technology to facilitate teacher learning? Bransford concluded that good educational software and teacher-support tools, developed with full understanding of the principles of learning, have not yet become the norm, and that the ILIT committee's deliberations about these questions would benefit the educational community.

Nora Sabelli, University of Texas at Austin, followed Bransford's remarks with a short presentation on creating partnerships in K-12 education that bring research and practice together. At the start of her talk, she said that there is a consensus that the problems facing the public are in urgent need of attention and that existing basic research on how people learn, if used properly, could make a big difference in addressing those problems. However, in her view, the results of the basic research must be linked more strongly to the implementation issues raised in applying such research, and until these links are established, the potential for using the basic research to improve K-12 education will remain unrealized.

Sabelli said that education presents special challenges to creating such partnerships because there is no private sector research in education, and there is limited capacity to conduct the needed research at the state or local level. To address some of these challenges, she called for creating effective models for the interactions between technology, user-driven research (as defined by Stokes, 1997), and classroom practice. The creation of tools that embody those models requires partnerships and associated development cycles that are of sufficient scope to provide meaningful outcomes. The tools developed by the partnerships must be robust yet flexible enough to adapt to a wide range of conditions. Furthermore, she indicated that these tools should integrate tools and artifacts from other fields of knowledge; they should be driven by how they are used by teachers and students; and they should be capable of evolving.

In her closing remarks, Sabelli exhorted the audience to create partnerships that are like "fires and tornadoes," which will try to remain "alive" by modifying their environment to their needs, going around barriers, and replicating.

OPENING COMMENTS: PARTICIPANT OBSERVATIONS CONCERNING OBSTACLES AND CHALLENGES

Following the welcoming remarks, the participants were encouraged to begin a frank discussion about their respective communities as the first step toward building a common vocabulary, and thereby fostering more mutual understanding and respect of each other's domains. The conversation was facilitated by David Sibbet, president of the Grove Consultants International, who translated participants' remarks into a visual representation of connections, alliances, barriers, and opportunities. The visual representation of this activity, admittedly challenging to interpret in its static state without the benefit of watching its creation, is available on the project's website, <http://www.nrcilit.org>.

Participants shared the challenges they face within their sector, the opportunities on the horizon that better use of information technology promises, and a realistic explanation of how success is measured and rewarded within their own communities. This activity was undertaken to foster a clearer understanding of ineluctable divergence, dawning convergence, and possible partnership and facilitation among the three main communities. The honest exchange generated a range of issues for the ILIT committee to consider. The conversation also prompted colleagues to suggest other organizations, companies, researchers, and educators to engage in this process. Many of the comments are summarized below.

Identifying Fundamental Community Differences

A participant offered initial comments, describing a "caricature" of the separate, sometimes competing, and certainly diverse nature of the different communities—learning sciences, education, and the IT industry:

- Learning scientists write grants and papers, conduct research, earn tenure (or not), and get promoted (or not).
- Educators teach students, make lesson plans, communicate with parents and administrators.
- The IT industry makes products and delivers shareholder value.

He added that each group holds unproductive myths about the others. For instance, educators are tired of experts telling them what to do. They have been through that time and again. Educators and learning scientists often do not trust industry. Claims of intuitive, easy-to-use equipment prove untrue, while quality of service is too often lacking. Learning scientists often perceive that educators are resistant to change, and industry does not take the time to understand the learning scientists' research findings. Few educators or industry representatives read the journals in which learning scientists publish, while educators or learning scientists may not follow industry news and are unlikely to be proficient with technology or inventive enough to see the potential of technological tools. Another participant commented that because the rewards in industry are very different from those in academia and teaching, industry can be a difficult partner. Industry is rewarded for making money, thus it concentrates on who is in charge, how many students the products will reach, and what will make money. These broad differences suggest different strategies, goals, and information-seeking activities, and they point to the myriad obstacles facing the ILIT committee as it attempts to build a coalition among these sectors.

Opinions from the K-12 Sector

A K-12 educator noted that education was in the middle of the diagram constructed on the whiteboard during this conversation. He thought this was both ironic and accurate, as education often appears to be squeezed by the other stakeholders. On one side, the learning sciences community provides the latest strategies or tools based on its research, but these findings may be valid for only a year or two until the next "breakthrough." This speaker asserted that, by necessity, many educators have "desensitized" themselves to this sector's contributions and continue to do what their experience tells them is best for helping children learn. The speaker also felt that, on the other side, educators think the technology industry "comes in and feeds off of them for a while" and then disappears.

He acknowledged that this was an unfair generalization of the role of both of these communities, but an historical perspective tended to validate educators' disgruntlement. Finally, he commented that leaders within the education community itself found it challenging to change these impressions. For instance, he and his colleagues were attempting to impress upon professionals within their sphere of influence that there is a constantly evolving outlook on pedagogy stemming from learning sciences research, and that an awareness of this research should be among the professional demands of teachers.

Building on the previous speaker's view from the "front lines," a learning scientist noted that the biggest resistance from classroom teachers comes because they have not been engaged in goal setting. It was her experience that when teachers find a new product or educational strategy that makes a difference, they will adopt it instantly, especially if they encounter it early in the school year. This participant encouraged the ILIT committee, within its work, to treat teachers as true customers rather than as mere conduits to students. Teachers are the human agents in the classroom. Another K-12 representative added that the conversation seemed to imply that education was the point of resistance and that another, stronger body could "empower" it, rather than treating it as a partner in the process.

A K-12 educator questioned what he had in common with the university professors who were present at the symposium—many of whom were considered part of the "education" domain as he was. He represented a public school district with 11,000 students, 97 percent of whom are ethnic minorities, and 85 percent of whom are poor. His goal and that of other urban educators is to make sure that these children have access to higher education and to employ technology to achieve that.

Another participant from the K-12 sector offered a concrete appeal to the technology community. She stated that, beyond purchasing licenses, there is currently nothing that documents what students do every time they touch the computer; there is no system that specifically collects that kind of data. Although web-browser cookies are collected (documenting websites students visit), teachers and administrators are not able to integrate data about what sites students are viewing so that they can build on students' interests.

Finally, another person with ties to both the learning sciences and technology communities commented that if any progress is to be made, participants should understand that education is not monolithic. There are policy makers at the state or district levels who have considerable clout. There are administrators, students, and parents who must be courted. Most of all, there are the teachers who must be persuaded and engaged to bring their experiences to the partnership. Understanding the roles, perspectives, and interests of these various players should be a key part of the ILIT study, and a similar exercise should be attempted for the learning sciences and industry communities as well.

Potential Goals for Technology in the Classroom

At one point in the symposium, a computer scientist thought it pertinent to offer three possible reasons for fully integrating technology into K-12 education, and he challenged the group to decide which of these would be the focus for the ILIT project:

1. *Technology as a skill.* Just as other practical courses, such as keyboarding and cooking, are offered to prepare students for their future, using technology skillfully should be included in the K-12 curriculum.

2. *Computers as tools for learning and discovery.* The education, research, and IT communities must grapple with how to integrate technology into the educational process so that it fundamentally changes teaching and learning, enabling knowledge creation and development.

3. *Understanding technology fundamentals.* Information technology will be with today's children for the rest of their lives, and the dramatic changes exhibited through the four waves of the Internet that occurred in the past 30 years will continue to change over the next 30 years, probably at a faster pace. Students must understand the fundamentals so that their learning keeps pace with technological developments, regardless of how they choose to spend their lives.

He recognized that most of the conversation up to this point had centered on the second goal, but suggested that the others were also important for the committee to consider. Another researcher commented that it would be imperative that prospective clients for any of the above goals be consulted in order to prioritize the goals.

Another participant commented that the discussion thus far had centered on formal education. This person encouraged ILIT colleagues to consider building coalitions among the large set of informal educational communities: youth-serving organizations and after-school programs, for example, as well as cultural institutions, libraries, museums, archives, etc.

As part of this discussion of goals and vision, another participant questioned what kind of infrastructure the community must construct to accomplish its mission. He lamented the lack of a solid "implementation science" or "implementation art," whereby successful projects could be scaled up to affect a larger share of the educational community. He commented that this would require a "start-to-finish" or "end-to-end" objective, a task that educators appear unequipped to imagine at this time, nor did he think that there was sufficient technical infrastructure to support creating such a model. He envisioned a model that would include indicators of success or areas for improvement besides those commonly used (i.e., test scores). Educators hear everyone clamoring for results, he said, but the ILIT project should be very articulate about who the partners are, what they can offer, and whose lives will be enriched and how.

Continuing that line of thought, a learning scientist stated that the nation needs innovation and a new science of implementation that takes into account assessments of merit for both individual and organizational performance—indicators other than standard scores and more traditional assessment measures. He also called for more thoughtful, principled consideration of the nature of an IT infrastructure that would be sustainable, particularly by under-resourced organizations. He suggested that capitalizing on application service providers, movements to make "opensource" code available (e.g., <http://sourceforge.net/>), and other trends might be more effective than assuming that the dominant consumer models are the best strategy.

The Accountability Specter

Many participants acknowledged the increasing importance of accountability that is currently engulfing K-12 education. One cognitive scientist remarked that, in her dealings with teachers and administrators, she took care to explain the basis of her work, her background in cognitive science, and why the strategy she was proposing seemed promising. However, she noted that, increasingly, the only language that really registers with K-12 leaders is the language of results. Given ongoing national, local, and state efforts to require schools to show improved test scores or risk penalties such as having their students removed or awarded vouchers to attend other schools, this emphasis on testing seems to be a persistent pressure under which educators now must work. She cautioned ILIT committee members to consider questions of accountability carefully throughout their deliberations.

Considering Context

A colleague in a large university system was compelled to remind others that context is extremely important in addressing the problem of improving learning with information technology. As she noted, in some cases the university system is either more or less important than the state education bureaucracy. She said that instead of worrying about the differences in vocabulary and perspectives among the three sectors, participants should recognize that what actually matters is the view among the different education stakeholders. She posited that current trends indicate that members of some state boards of education are less interested in developing empowered learners than in teaching students phonics and the conventional algorithms for computation. The current thinking of the information technology and learning sciences communities represented at the symposium and the instructional materials actually purchased by the states are worlds apart. She mentioned that some states, such as California, are adopting only software that teaches children conventional algorithms. Even materials that many educators and learning scientists considered mathematically accurate and pedagogically superior were not adopted because they appeared to require "too much intelligence" on the part of the teacher. She continued that materials that had well-developed artificial intelligence (AI) components built into them for algebra were not even considered because of perceived obstacles—they were delivered in a technological format, students could not take them home to do homework, and so on. Finally, she believed that the discussion so far had wholly neglected the contexts in which the diverse communities must work to accomplish what the symposium participants seemed to agree needs to be accomplished.

An administrator identified another mismatch: between the traditional educational infrastructure or establishment and another, wholly different system that might perhaps better suit efforts to build an integrated technology. He commented that the old educational establishment, particularly the university structure of incentives, budgets, and the flow of money, is out of alignment with new visions of education and must be transformed (see, for example, NRC, 1999d). Technology has the potential to reduce distance and time dramatically, in both the geographic and organizational sense, and ideas can be implemented quickly. In short, he posited that information technology applications are out of sync with the predominant, current institutional infrastructures. However, another participant challenged this statement. He claimed that often the technology falls radically short of enabling users to achieve the visions and aspirations it promised, so a new paradigm seems premature.

Frank Reflections on Past Efforts to Incorporate Technology into the Classroom

As part of this discussion, a computer science professor commented that he had attempted to use technology in college-level teaching but found the cost-benefit ratio for both students and faculty to be quite unclear. He acknowledged that we have reached the point where technology is doubling things that matter, specifically computing power, and this means that IT is finally positioned to be truly useful to educators if only they could understand how best to apply it. However, he reminded others of the skepticism that past efforts to harness the power of technology in the classroom had generated within the education community. He noted that the early hyperbole about the potential of IT had resulted in the introduction of technology into K-12 education at a very rapid rate and a very great cost. Despite valiant attempts by educators to transform teaching and learning at these grade levels, IT had often proved more trouble than educators thought it was worth. Furthermore, there is very little research evidence to support the claim that IT actually improves learning outcomes (President's Committee of Advisors on Science and Technology, 1997), and a growing cynicism among educators about its promise (see, for example, Cuban, 2001). This, he cautioned, is one of the obstacles facing the ILIT committee.

Technology Generating New Knowledge

An academic with strong industry ties remarked that the semiotic[7] dimension of information technology has been generating new knowledge about teaching and learning; modern computational media now allow educators and researchers to change representational infrastructures in mathematics especially (Kaput and Roschelle, 1998), and representational infrastructures then change what it means to know, that is, they change the very nature of knowledge, learning, and cognition. He continued that he thought that applications of information technology were becoming out of sync with this burgeoning new knowledge. He cautioned that, as stake-

---

[7]A general philosophical theory of signs and symbols that deals especially with their function in both artificially constructed and natural languages and comprises syntactics, semantics, and pragmatics. Merriam-Webster, Inc. (1991). *Webster's Ninth New Collegiate Dictionary*. Springfield, MA: Author

holders consider using IT to improve the delivery of learning, they should also question the kinds of knowledge that students should be learning. Much cognitive work has examined these new forms of knowledge, learning, and representational infrastructures. He cited the work of symposium participant Alex Repenning, who has developed AgentSheets as a software application to provide end-user programmable agent-based modeling systems for educational use, which simply modeled dynamical systems that previously could not be modeled by traditional representational infrastructures, such as algebra or arithmetic or even coordinate graphing systems (Repenning, Ioannidou, and Zola, 2000).

Audience

One participant invited the others at the symposium to talk seriously about who the learners are that the ILIT committee wants to help. He speculated that those in attendance would differ in their answers to that question. He added that his commitment to improving learning with information technology stemmed from caring deeply about how these different strategies will improve the lives of students, teachers, and parents who work hard every day to improve education in the United States. He realized that there are other audiences as well.

A Caution about Developing Too Common a Language

Finally, one participant cautioned that trying to develop a common language could turn out to be a nonconstructive exercise. It could conceal fundamentally important facets that distinguish the different communities. He warned colleagues to be aware of this paradox.

EXEMPLARS: IT CAN BE DONE

The symposium included presentations by representatives from four projects that have successfully used information technologies to achieve significant goals. These projects all involved partnerships that required the kind of bridging work the ILIT committee would like to highlight and promote nationally for further achievement in improving learning with information technology.

LemonLINK

Barbara Allen and Darryl LaGace shared their insight in developing and managing Project LemonLINK, based in Lemon Grove, California, which focuses on high-speed connectivity; equitable, adequate access to resources; development of web-based instructional tools; and ongoing professional development for teachers.

LemonLINK is a Connected Learning Community model built around an application service provider (ASP) for the entire community. Using server-based computing, thin-client technology, and a high-speed cable modem network that makes the latest technology available to those who can least afford it, the Lemon Grove School District has become one of the first to become an application service provider for an entire community. By turning the thin clients into a simple appliance that anyone can operate, as well as making access to the latest programs and educational resources available, LemonLINK enables businesses and families in the community to bridge the digital divide. This model is one example of an affordable computing device without costly maintenance or software upgrades. A user-friendly, web-based interface acts as a common portal, linking the city to the educational community and ensuring that families throughout the community have an equitable advantage to informational technology access.

The heart of the project has been the creation of a Connected Learning Community through business and government partnerships to develop a unique infrastructure that connects all schools and the city via microwave and fiber-optic technologies. The network's architect is Darryl LaGace, Lemon Grove School District's director of information systems, who envisioned a connected learning community in which the school district serves as the communication hub for an entire community. What makes the system unique is the use of a microwave tower, located at the district office. Each school and city facility in turn has its own microwave and/or fiber-optic link and can access the programs needed from workstations in classrooms and offices. The wide-area network (WAN) provides enough bandwidth to support a full duplex Ethernet connection from 100 MB to 1 GB to each location. In turn, all district sites have been wired with fiber-optic backbone, hubs, and switches. Because every classroom is connected to the network, all the computers in those classrooms are connected to the Internet. All city government facilities have been wired including City Hall, the Fire Department, Public Works, the Recreation Department, the

Community Center, Teen Center and the Senior Center. Construction of the sophisticated microwave WAN began in 1993.

Significant business partnerships have been the key to making the Connected Learning Community vision a reality. The system has attracted the attention of a number of technology, telecommunications, and software companies such as Microsoft, Compaq, Cox Communications, Cisco, Citrix, Bell and Howell, Computer Curriculum Corporation, Communications Systems Group, and Wyse Technology. These firms, along with many others, have assisted Lemon Grove in further development to expand the network into homes in the community.

Union City, New Jersey

Fred Carrigg and students Steven Perez and José Marrero talked about the transformation of the Union City, New Jersey, public schools from a failing system to an exemplar.

Union City, New Jersey, is located in Hudson County, directly across the Hudson River from Manhattan. With 60,000 residents in 1.4 square miles, it is the most densely populated city in the United States. The predominant ethnic makeup of Union City is Cuban, though recent arrivals from the Caribbean and Central and South America, as well as longtime Italian residents, add to the diversity of the city's population. Of the 10,500 students in the district's 11 schools, 93 percent are Latino, 70 percent of whom do not speak English at home. Thirty-four percent of the students are enrolled in the district's bilingual/ESL program. The Brookings Institute classified Union City as one of the 92 most impoverished communities in the United States; 27.5 percent of Union City's children live below the poverty line, and 84 percent receive free or reduced-priced lunches.

In 1989, the Union City schools failed in 44 out of the 52 categories that the State of New Jersey uses to determine the effectiveness of school districts. The schools were failing in areas such as student attendance, drop-out rates, and scores on standardized tests, and as a result they were threatened with state takeover. Like many urban districts, Union City was also facing many obstacles to correcting these deficiencies, including language barriers, parents with limited formal education, and students with little incentive to stay in school.

Rather than lose local control of the school district, however, Union City decided to face these challenges head on and drastically reform the entire educational system. This entailed formulating and implementing a five-year Corrective Action Plan that drastically reformed the entire educational system through the following changes: extending most classes in subject areas to 120-minute periods in elementary and middle schools and 80-minute periods in high schools; increasing in-service training for teachers from 8 hours a year to 40 hours; refurbishing buildings, replacing windows, and painting classrooms and hallways; replacing individual student desks with cooperative learning tables; and replacing textbooks for individual students with class libraries.

Union City chose to implement the reforms in the elementary classrooms first, then add classes year by year until reform reached every grade level. This decision meant that no student schooled in a reformed learning environment had to face the former method of instruction when he or she entered a new grade. Furthermore, the inevitable headaches that arise during renovations and the first years of new curricula were kept to a manageable scale. It also meant that the District was able to take the lessons learned from each successive implementation and apply them toward easing the transition in subsequent years.

In addition to curriculum reforms, substantial increases in the district's operating budget played a critical role in Union City's efforts. Over the past eight years, the budget for the Union City School District increased from $37.8 million in 1989 to $126 million in 2001 as a direct result of equitable school funding legislation, known in New Jersey as the Quality Education Act (QEA).

Beginning in 1993, Union City also made a deliberate decision to invest substantially in technology resources. The city did this largely out of equity considerations, believing that urban students would once again risk falling drastically behind suburban students if they did not have access to state-of-the-art technological resources. The district built fiber backbones in each of its 11 schools. Approximately 85 percent of the 3.500 instructional computers—those in classrooms, media centers, and computer labs—are part of a district-wide network that connects the schools, two public libraries, the city hall, and the local daycare center to the central office servers through T-1 lines. With a ratio of four students per computer, Union City is now one of the most wired urban school districts in the United States.

Learning Technologies in Urban Schools, Designing for Instructional Change

The Chicago City Science program was presented by Barbara Watkins, principal of James McCosh Elementary School (and now chief education officer of the Chicago public schools); Irene DaMota, principal of Roberto Clemente High School; and Louis Gomez, associate professor of learning sciences at Northwestern University. The Chicago City Science program consists of two partnerships. One partnership involved the Center for Learning Technologies in Urban Schools (LeTUS),[8] and middle school curriculum development teams at McCosh. The second partnership involved LeTUS and high school curriculum development teams at Clemente through the Math, Science, and Technology Academy (MSTA).[9]

The goals of the LeTUS-McCosh partnership were to develop innovations in science teaching that conform to an accountability system focused on mathematics and literacy; to integrate technology with instruction; to initiate collaborations in which teachers work together on instruction; and to develop leadership from within the school. The goals of the LeTUS-Clemente partnership were to generate ideas for developing high-performing schools and to building a learning community. To achieve these goals, the partnerships had to resolve conflicts between the goals of the research project and those of the districts and find a way to fit the project into crowded instructional agendas.

The LeTUS-McCosh partnership is credited with helping increase students' scores on the Iowa Test of Basic Skills (ITBS). Between the partnership's inception in 1995 and 1999, the mathematics scores on the ITBS for all students at McCosh have risen about 19 percent, while their scores in reading have risen more than 15 percent. Lessons from the McCosh partnership include the recognition that the partnerships must focus on developing the professional community of teachers within the

---

[8]A National Science Foundation funded center with a partnership between Chicago public schools, Detroit public schools, Northwestern University, and the University of Michigan that forms collaborations with urban schools, designs project-based science curricula, develops interactive computing technologies, and supports systemic education reform.

[9]A partnership between Chicago Public Schools, Chicago City Colleges, and four-year colleges and universities with the goal of improving teacher professional development, curriculum, and student academic achievement in mathematics, science, and technology education in grades 7-14.

school if they expect to have a school-wide impact; partners must be carefully selected to ensure that the program remains coherent; and long-term partnerships tend not only to generate new research questions but to offer the means with which to answer them.

The experience of the Clemente partnership produced two important lessons: For the desired learning communities to take root, they need an instructional focus; and team-based curriculum planning changes teaching and learning practices. Furthermore, the prestige of a partnership can also encourage even tightly controlled school bureaucracies to allow some latitude in the design of the program. The LeTUS-Clemente partnership is credited with helping increase student performance in reading and mathematics. Students who were performing below their grade level before entering the program made an average grade-level gain in mathematics of 0.88, whereas similar students who were not in the program gained only 0.51 grade levels. The corresponding gains in reading are 1.20 grade levels versus 0.42 grade levels. The differentials in grade-level gains for students performing above grade level are 2.03 versus 0.79 in mathematics and 1.74 versus 0.14 in reading.

The SimCalc/UMass-Dartmouth/Texas Instruments Partnership

James Kaput of the University of Massachusetts, Dartmouth, explained the goals of the SimCalc project, which aims to introduce powerful mathematical ideas to young children by using techniques that tap into their natural abilities. SimCalc is based on the premise that technology provides essential means to restructure curriculum in order to democratize access to important and powerful ideas; build much more longitudinal coherence between the early and the later years of education; focus on the growth of big ideas and their roots in everyday human experience; crack the formalism barrier by providing multiple ways of working with mathematical ideas, using the full range of human linguistic, visualization, and cognitive capacities; increase efficiency by teaching several important ideas simultaneously; and bring mathematics taught in K-12 schools out of the nineteenth century and into the twenty-first century.

The SimCalc Project began in 1993 as a National Science Foundation (NSF) research project to democratize access for students in grades 6-13 to the mathematics of change and variation, including the ideas underlying calculus. The initial project was based on prior work by Kaput and Ricardo

Nemirovsky at TERC in the late 1980s, and eventually evolved into two separate partnerships—one to conduct research and another to address commercial issues.

To achieve the goal of increasing the accessibility of the mathematics of change and variation, the project developed and field-tested new software and curriculum materials that incorporated interactive simulations and visualization tools. It also needed to confront resistance based on beliefs and practices regarding the nature of mathematics—who might learn it and how it might be learned—and the curriculum structures built into American education and assessment systems that the project needed to address.

The initial concept was desktop-centric, but it became clear that personal handheld devices were a better approach despite the limited programming tools for calculators available at the time. The pace of change in technology also created a tension between continuing development for the large number of older models already in place versus adopting the newest models with superior features.

Between 1993 and 1996, the SimCalc project software and instructional materials were successfully piloted with populations of inner-city and at-risk students in Massachusetts, New Jersey, New York, Michigan, and California. This phase showed that mainstream students could learn the ideas and skills embodied in SimCalc. The project also investigated related issues of learning, component software development, interface design, and the learning differences in observing simulated motion versus observing physical motion.

The second phase of the project lasted from 1996 to 2000. It addressed several issues: how to integrate the ideas and materials generated on the first phase into grade 6-13 curricula while respecting the current accountability system in schools; how to build functional software for platforms that schools can afford; and how to build upon and expand the existing capacities of teachers, teacher-educators, schools, and districts.

The third phase, which started in 2000, consists of two efforts: developing assessment systems that provide reliable data on student learning, and developing commercial products in partnership with Texas Instruments. This phase also includes investigating the affordances and constraints of wireless networks connecting many kinds of devices, and discovering how experiences with physical devices can feed into and influence the learning of mathematical ideas.

2
Symposium Activity: Forging a Common Language, Building Alliances

ACTIVITY BACKGROUND AND SCOPE

As desired, the symposium attracted people from the three distinct domains—education, industry, and the learning sciences. Many participants were contributors to more than one domain. On the second day, symposium participants self-assigned into four breakout groups[1] to consider three design problems (two groups discussed the same challenge). The symposium organizers chose to provide each group with the broadest design problem idea (i.e., a project title), but not to dictate any other requirement; this would allow the participants to struggle with their assumptions about each problem and to rethink conditions for addressing it. Facilitators were asked to note the context, product, and process undertaken by their group members. The following summarizes the discussions at these three-hour breakout sessions.

---

[1] The composition of the working groups was verified to assure that all three domains were adequately represented.

Scenario 1:
Creating an Advanced Placement Calculus Course for a Rural High School

Jeremy Roschelle, SRI International, and Uri Treisman, University of Texas at Austin, facilitated this breakout group.

Context: This breakout group devised its own context from which to launch its discussions: In Texas, there are 500 rural high schools serving 7 percent of the students. These are small high schools that cannot offer much math and science. About 280,000 students are taking math at any given time in the schools. The goal is to enroll 12,000 students per year in calculus. State policy requires equalizing opportunities for these students. Many are poor. It is an ethnically mixed demographic. Historically, most of these schools have only taught algebra and have no experience teaching calculus. A growing Spanish-speaking population wants AP calculus to be available, and a strategy must be found to serve these schools. The ultimate goal is to achieve a higher rate of acceptance to college for these students.

Funding for the technology infrastructure consists of approximately $150 million for hardware, which has been invested in numerous yet makeshift ways. Some schools have expensive videoconferencing and some thin client-run equipment. Most districts have a T-1 line into the principal's office. Very few classrooms are connected, but computer use is growing. Most people have a 28K modem connection at home.

Texas already provides some professional development for teachers, at least five days during the summer and some days during the school year. However, the math teachers have determined that they need fifteen days of professional development and have formally requested at least these days be made available.

One-third of the math teachers are teaching the subject without a good math background. About 10 of the 500 schools are success models and are already providing calculus. Some of these schools succeeded mainly by coordinating the effort from middle school onward—AP calculus is not treated as an isolated activity. In other cases, the achievement is attributable to determined individual teachers who persevered on their own.

Rural Texans are increasingly interested in using the Internet to gain access to products and services, and the state is investing in rural connectivity. By 2003, the Texas state legislature is going to issue a request for proposals to build a system. The governor wants several solutions offered to promote competition. The governor also wants districts to control some of the dollars. The state wants the systems to start being delivered by 2004.

The breakout group devised a framework for discussion: plan of action, likely barriers, the role of technology, and assessable measures of achievement of the project goals. One participant suggested the discussion concentrate on a challenge faced by administrators and educators in Texas before the group attempted to grapple with the goal to provide AP calculus to students in rural areas.

Product: The group realized that this problem was too complex to tackle in its entirety in the allotted time and therefore decided to consider some specific dimensions of the problem. The group attempted to construct a Request For Proposals (RFP) whereby successful bidders were allowed to learn from their work, to create revisions, and to develop the necessary technology over the course of the project, using as much of the existing equipment as possible. There was some debate about whether the RFP should ask for a single AP calculus course or require a longer-term effort by districts and the provider that would begin at the middle school level and refashion how students are prepared for high-level mathematics.

Process: All the participants felt that the pivotal opening strategy would be to understand the environment in which the technology would be used. The group immediately rejected the stated goal of "creating an AP course"; instead, most of them agreed that the real task was to build something far more robust, something "that had a verticalness to it." The group wanted a system that would support teachers at different levels and thereby build a pedagogical infrastructure that would lead seamlessly to offering an AP calculus course for which both students and teachers would be prepared.

Because the group had begun by generally agreeing that an infrastructure was required before introducing AP calculus, the discussion focused on the realities of the schools: the needs and requirements, the challenges for teachers, and the need to support them in learning and performance. Many participants identified difficult challenges during this conversation.

First, some members stated that although IT has offered advances in many domains, it has not yet done so for calculus because of its many mathematical symbols and the free-response questions on the AP examination. Participants from industry also pointed out how important it was to understand capacity in different learning environments. Many of the things academics and learning scientists really value—such as generating a large proportion of students prepared to take calculus or developing many customized learning options for students—might not be realistically possible. Lower-end, more generic options might be necessary instead.

Tensions between the use of calculators versus the Web were noted. Although participants naturally envisioned a computer-based solution, the AP course requires calculators, not computers. Yet the group did not consider how calculators would be part of the solution. Furthermore, even as some people asserted that the system obviously should be web-based, one participant claimed that some data indicate that web-based AP calculus is actually not as effective as "real" AP calculus with a teacher.

Educators emphasized that the assets of education are people. Any strategy adopted to incorporate calculus into the curriculum must be designed in a way to retain teachers. The educators explained further that Advanced Placement has thrived because it is an elitist course that enables students who are good learners to take a university-level course in a high school setting before they go to college. However, in an age of increasing accountability and increasing teacher shortages, the incentive for teachers and schools to take on the most rigorous, demanding work is unclear when, in the short term, they will be judged only by how many students take the exam and do well.

The idea of using IT assessment tools was appealing to the group: It would allow teachers to assign better targeted and more appropriate work and would give them the help they need in grading and evaluating the work. IT was also viewed as a means for helping students, teachers, and other stakeholders evaluate strategies to improve student learning and teaching. This point led the group to consider ways to increase and facilitate information sharing via technology. If a school is to succeed in such an ambitious goal as establishing a new course, there must be constructive leadership that encourages people to talk openly about student work. If the kinds of communication that technology supports do not assist that local leadership in such efforts, the mismatch could be damaging for calculus and other areas of the curriculum. Taking the time to understand the leadership and organizational structures in these Texas schools would be critical.

Some privacy issues were raised: Who would have authority and access to watch what teachers do? Who would control data about individual students? How would the necessary iteration and improvement process be interpreted as implementation unfolds? Furthermore, would these new technology-based assessment tools be defensible, both politically and in the courts? These questions emphasized how critical it is to understand the complex social environment before introducing such fluid, flexible data mining. Who has access to what data and how the data might be used are complicated issues. The group struggled with how to change the oftentimes-negative image of assessment into one that is constructive for both teachers and students.

Participants from the learning sciences community commented that, although a lot is known about learning in general, the particulars of learning in this specific discipline (calculus) would be important in this project. And the experts appeared to agree that much work remains to be done. What are the organizing principles that underlie the teaching and learning of calculus? In general, the facilitators noted that the cognitive scientists required a great deal of evidence and exercised a lot of professional caution in the discussions. However, educators and policy makers must often act without what a cognitive scientist would consider sufficient evidence. This difference in perspective raises a potentially serious challenge to developing cross-disciplinary partnerships.

One person offered a challenge to the breakout group, which mirrored on a small scale the challenges that the ILIT committee is likely to encounter as it works to bring these groups together. This participant commented that the goal of the AP course seemed to be to enable students to pass the AP examination. He questioned whether society should be harnessing the Internet and all of those other technology tools just so more people can have the opportunity to pass the AP calculus exam. Is this a good purpose? Do we want to take something like the AP examination, which has been part of the traditional educational culture, and put it into a more flexible and dynamic learning environment? He suggested that maybe educators need to change their thinking about the purpose of taking an AP calculus class.

Another tension centered on the question of time scales. Rather than developing a longer-term, more ambitious strategy, this group concentrated on what could be done in the next couple of years. But one key element of the long-range view is that 10 years from now, the role that teachers play will almost certainly have changed. Teachers may become student motivators, and other resources such as experts may be available only online or as specialists in one domain. The job descriptions for the teachers of the future are going to look very different from what teachers do in classrooms today. Those changing expectations present an inherent tension between the current emphasis on curricular management and the support system needed to build this new community. The technical, sociological, and educational challenges must all be addressed simultaneously.

This group very quickly recognized the multifaceted challenges of the design problem of building a real system that is going to affect real students.

Scenario 2:
Enhancing Literacy in Children: Reading to Learn

Marilyn Adams, BBN Technologies, and Tom Landauer, University of Colorado, facilitated this breakout group.

Context: One of the participants in this breakout session presented the following challenge:

The governor declared, "Here is what I want. Imagine that I have unlimited resources. I want to 'enhance literacy in children' and develop their skills to 'read to learn.' I have been advised that you are the experts best able to tackle this challenge. Tell me what to do. Offer a convincing proposal. Make it practical. Make it usable. Make it address this issue publicly and be tailored for individual needs, conceivable within our decentralized public school system, and accepted and supported by both parents and teachers."

The group began its discussion by asking each participant to suggest the most urgent and important issue facing literacy education that could be addressed with technology. The participants introduced themselves but did not explicitly address their biases or assumptions. They generally thought that the real promise—the excitement inherent in information technology—was its potential to enhance and deepen the literacy of students. In this group's estimation, IT could not only close the functional literacy[2] gap but also increase children's analytical literacy.[3] IT could enable students not only to read stories more capably, but also to think and interpret while reading in other subject areas such as algebra or science. The ambitious goal would be to enable the definition of literacy to evolve to a more sophisticated level.

---

[2]Functional literacy refers to the ability of an individual to use reading, speaking, writing, and computational skills in everyday life situations.

[3]Analytical literacy refers to the ability of an individual to use analytical skills to question and respond to such elements as perspective, purpose, effect, and relevance of what they read and write.

Product: Following the governor's challenge, the breakout group members selected a problem area for which to "make an invention"—the development of literacy for middle school students. Participants felt that this was an area of critical importance because it involved serving the needs of adolescents, an age group where ever-widening gaps in literacy develop, often with irreparable consequences. Some children need basic reading support, while others read adequately but need help integrating or advancing their understanding of the material. The group wished to guide all children in more active thinking and engagement with the text.

Furthermore, some asserted that the commercial market was not serving this age level adequately, perhaps because it *is* such a diffuse community. However, the group reasoned that this very neglect made the issue ripe for addressing through some complex technological assistance.

Another strategy to improve literacy was to use technology to remedy the dreaded "fourth grade slump," when reading progress often stagnates or even declines. The group thought that the real utility of reading is its contribution to a person's ability to engage with other people and with his or her society and culture, and thus achieve success in life. Developing a technology-enabled or -enhanced system to aggressively tackle the decline would be vitally important. The breakout group thought that any system should address all the challenges together and try to remedy them simultaneously. The group spent 15 minutes to allow everyone to suggest a component of the system, which over the project cycle of three years, might be integrated into a strategy to confront the problem.

Almost everyone had a product or component to suggest. One of the facilitators remarked that the complementarity and range of products were impressive. While the likelihood of "solving" the problem was unknown, participants' suggestions appeared to be positive steps toward meeting the challenge. The group was enthusiastic about the idea that a demonstration project was not only possible but probably necessary for the literacy community, which has not been broadly exposed to how IT tools could work in that domain. The group, however, did not abandon its eagerness to celebrate books and emphasized that IT would not replace books but increase their accessibility.

The following ideas were generated for the proposed demonstration project. Some already exist in whole or in part, while others are "blue sky" proposals.

- **A Needs Assessment Proposal.** Participants encouraged the drafting of a proposal to gather data from customers and stakeholders in the literacy issue—students, teachers, parents, the public, politicians, others—about their needs, the resources currently used, and a wish list of improvements or suggestions.

- **A Human-Computer Interaction (HCI), Participatory Design.** A common fault of the past has been that it is technologists who identify the components needed to manage problems (NRC, 1997), including problems such as how to enhance literacy. Participants were vocal in their critique of that paradigm. They were eager to encourage engaging the educational partners in the process by working with them to assess their problems and their resources, and by partnering with them to help build and employ information technology that will be useful in tackling the challenge.

- **Writing Assessment Tools.** Develop technological tools to assess comprehension and expression in free-form writing. Tools that could assess comprehension and give feedback to students (and their teachers) could motivate, assess, and track students' progress and drive a cyclical improvement of the entire system.

- **An Online Reading Adviser.** Construct a sophisticated web-based program or software package to make reading more enjoyable and encourage more reading. This system would offer each student suggestions for further reading based on his or her past experience, just as commercial websites recommend new books that are in line with a customer's past purchases and browsing behavior.

- **An Interactive, Text-Based, Oral, Reading-Based Tutor and Assessment Tool.** Make a product that would let students read aloud, correct them as necessary, and give advice for improvement. It should track progress over time for longitudinal assessment and tutorial feedback.

- **A Network Learning Community for Education of Teachers.** This network could link teachers who are proficient with new technology or new methods with those who are not. This system could be particularly useful in cultivating expertise and confidence in teachers during their induction years, when they are most in danger of leaving the profession. Furthermore, in an age of "revolving-door" teachers, when many teachers move between grade levels or positions within or across schools and districts, a system such as this would help capture the skills and talents of those with the greatest experience so that the turnover does not unduly impede the educational process within the community. Technology should be able to help each cohort of new teachers adjust more quickly and be mentored more easily and effectively. After all, as one participant reminded the group, writing was intended to allow a faster and more voluminous passing of knowledge and skills between generations. Information technology should do no less.

- **A Network Learning Environment for New Teachers.** A variant of the above suggestion, this network would have collaborative and supportive activities for a virtual community of teachers. The network would enable teachers to work together to reach consensus on methods and tools to enhance student literacy.
- **A Change Management System for Principals.** This system would help principals learn what technology is available and how it is being used in classrooms/schools. It would provide a method for principals to share their opinions and knowledge for the benefit of others. This would encourage buy-in by principals for these new pedagogical tools and instructional styles and engender greater support for faculty innovation and experimentation.
- **Powerful, Persuasive Technologies Like Data Mining.** Data mining, the extraction of implicit, previously unknown, and potentially useful knowledge from data, is one of a variety of techniques used to identify and extract nuggets of information or decision-making knowledge from bodies of data so that they can be used in areas such as decision support, prediction, forecasting, and estimation (Witten and Frank, 2000). Data mining and other new tools that people in other domains find useful (such as CRM—Customer Relationship Management—tools by companies like Siebel) could be adapted for use in education. Databases could be constructed for both description and prescription. A complex database could keep track of what students have done, what they know, what their current skills and needs are, what is available for their continued progress, and what teachers can offer them. Technology has the power to help diagnose what the student or teacher needs and identify useful resources to correct deficiencies.
- **An Individualized Education Program (IEP).** While IEPs are currently mandated for certain segments of the school population, technology could be harnessed to provide an individualized instruction program for *every* student. This might be done by employing the tools used by marketers to create and send individualized ads based on the recipient's shopping history.
- **A Literacy Engagement Module.** A literacy engagement module connects students to the social context related to their reading interest. Participants encouraged drawing upon literacy activities such as social con-

texts, interaction with popular media, and interactive activities to engage students, while at the same time employing an assessment, response, and guidance module to adapt and extend the program capability.

- **Off-the-Shelf Technologies Adapted as Peer-Peer Tools.** Some participants suggested finding or creating tools that students can use among themselves to practice, use, and encourage literacy. Some in the group suggested that similar tools could be used to enable teachers to share their experiences and problems in literacy instruction.
- **A Spontaneous Speech and Vocabulary System.** This system could evaluate and track students' interests and capture their speech. It could assess each student's speech to identify problem areas and gauge vocabulary level. Such a system could employ new text understanding tools as well as the movement in XML and other ways to mark text to understand spoken text. And finally, the technology could be used to create a master model for developing literacy in children.
- **An Online Virtual Literacy Guild.** An online system filled with literary treasures would enable children to find and use literature they will enjoy. If this is a real-time system, teachers could use it as a resource.
- **Enabling Technologies for Learning Design Choices.** Participants were eager to consider how technology could allow learners to choose their own environment for learning, diagnostics, and prescriptions.
- **A Task and Tutoring System to Support Reading.** Breakout group participants were interested in having a real-time system that would support student readers or writers by making suggestions about tools or strategies that would increase proficiency.
- **Web-Based Scaffolds of Reference Materials.** Participants were eager to see a web-based scaffold of reference materials to support the growing writer and reader. One participant mentioned an example, "Just Read It." This is a collaborative magazine in which students' creative writing is published online and then read and discussed by friends and classmates.
- **Full-Scale Assessment.** Given the earlier plenary discussion regarding assessment and accountability, this group encouraged an assessment of an entire system to gauge its general effectiveness and to monitor progress on an iterative basis in order to provide a user-driven, fully tested design system within a three-year timeframe.
- **Equity.** The participants envisioned this system as a "collective parent" that would help equalize the differences between students' backgrounds by extending educational resources in space and time. Computing power customized for individual learning styles and needs would compensate for

variable preparedness when students are entering school and as they advance educationally.

- **Pilot Sites for Exploring Systemic Change.** Finally, the group was ambitious in suggesting a strategy for incorporating many of the above suggestions. They called for forging an integrated test bed of trial sites made up of principals, parents, teachers, students, and tools to be used for the iterative development of this large, comprehensive system.

Process: As with the previous breakout group, this group benefited from having participants who were comfortable in two or, in some instances, all three of the domains that were the focus of the symposium. Consequently, there was an affirmation that different perspectives will be needed to successfully address the goal of improving children's literacy. The group's discussion of the social and cultural aspects of the problem ranged from new literacy issues to the possibilities for collaboration through tools such as remote communication. Participants considered the tension between global connectivity and local isolation and between encouraging collaborative work and engaging each child's individual investment in his or her cognitive responsibilities. And, along with the social and contextual issues, not forgotten during the conversation was the buy-in needed from children, teachers, parents, and the larger educational system for the success of any solution.

The technology component of the discussion centered on individualization, not only to enable each student's independent pursuit of learning based on his or her interests, but also to construct a pedagogical IEP to customize learning for optimal results for every student. Information technologies were deemed sufficient to do this fairly well by means of data warehousing and aggregation. Other technical challenges were scaling problems and putting the components together.

Professional development and support were also critical. Technology that could enhance the diagnostic, prescriptive capabilities of the teacher would be very promising.

Across the whole educational system, the key component is effective assessment to serve as the driver of ideas and improvements. That is, technology should allow decision making based on a variety of data and then package data in ways that will be most useful and meaningful to people with different perspectives who will use them in different ways.

In conclusion, each participant had a rather different view of what was needed. Almost all had a suggestion, either completed or in mind, for solving the part of the problem that they saw. The consensus was that the group needed a comprehensive system that could incorporate the variety of suggestions offered, while allowing room for more ideas as well. One of the facilitators speculated that one reason the "product discussion" was so productive was that everyone felt free to offer his or her own component of the solution, and no suggestion appeared to conflict with another. What people contributed were strategies in which they were often already deeply engaged, so the activity resulted in enormous "handshakes," that is, participants recognized the complementarity of other group members' suggestions.

Scenario 3a:
Developing Environments for Learning Eighth Grade Science

Elizabeth Stage, University of California System, facilitated this breakout group.

Context: The goal was to improve science literacy for both students and teachers by encouraging more inquiry-based learning. One participant, reacting to what she perceived as the group's difficulty in conceiving a design problem to discuss, suggested a scenario centered on improving the climate and environment for teaching and learning science in the eighth grade. She challenged the group to offer advice to the people at the National Education Association (NEA) who have been assigned to design a web-based portal for their 2.5 million members. She asked group members to concentrate on the classroom channel of the portal, although discussants also identified other portals such as those for the community and for parents. She posed the following challenge:

How should the designers construct this portal so that users will come to a better understanding of eighth grade inquiry-based science? What is the role of information technology? How can one tackle the bigger challenge of large-scale implementation in concert with an ongoing learning community? What tools are needed? What is useful? How does one sort information? How does one adapt to the anticipated development of proficiency and expertise?

Other participants offered additional context. The middle school dimension likely includes students who have trouble reading, are not proficient in English, may have attitudinal blocks against science, and almost certainly are experiencing emotional and physical development issues. Likewise, many teachers may be totally unprepared to implement an inquiry-based science curriculum, mainly because they lack appropriate education in this subject. They may be teaching out of subject or they may simply not be up-to-date on current activities within the field.

Product: The group first attempted to design a portal where information could be disseminated. This concept evolved into building a web-based learning community. The group thought that many helpful resources currently exist and that broader dissemination would be a good first step in attempting to change the environment of middle school science. But group members did not reach consensus about how to build such a learning community. They acknowledged that many exemplars exist that could contribute to this community, and centralizing that knowledge would be valuable.

Process: The members of this breakout group began by identifying some resources that are information technology-based or have IT as a component that would likely be part of a portal. For example, some educational programs involve students tackling local environmental issues, such as testing local water sources, and then generating data tables to track changes in water quality. IT enables activities like videoconferencing so that students can talk with others who are physically, intellectually, and culturally distant from them. The technology also enables classes in different communities to collaborate on science experiments, sharing data and results to enrich each other's findings. Less ambitious examples included using the Web as a real-time access point to retrieve current information such as news on a fast-breaking science event. These examples and many others convey the range of uses for IT in the classroom. A portal could be one avenue by which schools share their programs in a centralized, organized, and multi-indexed way. Furthermore, the group envisioned the portal as a strategy to transform and deepen students' work, not simply to incorporate IT to improve the efficiency of the status quo.

Although identifying the resources would be daunting, the breakout group thought that it would probably be the easiest task in the process. Indexing and organizing resources so a teacher could determine how to use them in the classroom or a student could draw upon them for projects would be more difficult and more time-intensive. Quality control was also a major issue, with the definition of "quality" requiring a broad consensus. Many in the group emphatically agreed that the portal could not be static, and, therefore, the review process would have to be ongoing and evolutionary. Many participants wished to see gradations within the system so that teachers of varying skill levels could constructively access the portal. For example, some teachers might need a script with precise directions on how to implement a component, while others might only require a guidebook or general advice. Early adopters and classroom innovators should have an avenue to share their experience and to mentor peers.

Finally, many participants in this breakout session wanted a system that could track and highlight the evolution of IT examples from the initial introduction into a classroom or curriculum to IT as an inherent, embedded component enabling sophisticated scientific inquiry. As one member noted, the education community is only at a preliminary stage of dialogue right now. This means creating resources at the edge of innovation that might not have a lot of impact initially, but will help move the whole community toward a higher level of IT-based instruction. The task of the group was to find methods of encouraging people, through the tools themselves, to move from their current position to a more complex level.

To conclude, the facilitator observed a tremendous amount of patience and good-natured professional behavior throughout the session. The conversation oscillated between the specific problem of the portal design and the general concern that what is really needed is a learning community adept at addressing socio-cultural-textual challenges.

Scenario 3b:
Developing Environments for Learning Eighth Grade Science

Sharon Derry, University of Wisconsin, Madison, facilitated this breakout group.

Context: The facilitator suggested that the group keep in mind the challenge that most teachers of middle school science are not trained in science. The group further assumed that the science environment would be developed in a state where teachers would be furnished with state standards, and the accountability system would not necessarily be aligned with inquiry-based teaching. The group decided to focus on implementation strategies for a lower- or middle-income community.

The other group assigned to examine this subject area considered improving eighth grade science education in general. This group sought to design a learning environment for eighth grade that would not only help students learn science, but would also help teachers become better science teachers and learners.

Product: In addition to the constraints listed above, the group assumed that the teachers also do not have pedagogical content knowledge (Schulman, 1987) for this subject area. Many do not understand what "inquiry" is and therefore do not know how to teach an inquiry-based approach. Furthermore, many teachers without adequate science backgrounds do not enjoy teaching science. The group also acknowledged that the school administration and community do not always support new pedagogical approaches in the classroom.

Also because every state has different standards, devising a single generic strategy that would fulfill each set of standards could be quite difficult.

The introduction of technology would involve a lot of initial investments, but the breakout group members decided that if they were to act as leaders planning a solution, they would assume that computers would be available. They would also assume that money could be moved from one budget category to another and thus could be shifted toward the purchase of IT resources. After long debate, the participants also assumed that any computing power needed would be available because they were projecting their plans into the future. There was a consensus within the group that two years from now, educators could attempt IT-intensive pedagogy without worry, and five years from now, the question of sufficient computing power would be a non-issue. The group further thought that two years would be an appropriate timeframe for the development of a prototype that would demonstrate what good eighth grade science learning could look like.

The participants set some criteria for what the design should encompass: It should be cost-effective, resource rich, and incorporate all the possibilities provided by technology. It should be inquiry-based—that is, the curriculum should contain learning objectives that require not only factual recall, but also the ability to help users analyze data or information, synthesize new ideas, and test hypotheses. (The facilitator noted that there was no discussion about what "inquiry" meant, and she speculated that it likely meant different things to different participants.) Whatever was designed should not only address the students' needs, but also help change teachers' view of their role and of learning itself. The focus was on both student and teacher learning.

Process: The facilitator commented that it was a challenge for the group to decide on a focus. Initially, she asked everyone to offer his or her vision of the solution.

The group began by saying they did not want to focus on a particular curriculum or a particular content, but on what a big learning environment would look like—that is, they were committed to considering not just the local classroom, but the entire school and any place to which the school might network. Students might connect to other students in other learning environments and teachers to other teachers. Both groups might connect to experts. This kind of connectivity would allow the roles of teachers and students to evolve.

The participants wanted students to be empowered to take charge of their own learning. One strategy was to practice project-based learning grounded in the real world. The system would include built-in assessment. Students' work would generate continuous feedback, which would tell them what steps to take next. The teacher might be orchestrating the tactical framework, but students would make procedural decisions. Students should be doing real research that they design themselves, perhaps using multimedia to report their findings, and with end products that are real and concrete. Participants envisioned that students would also reflect about their learning to foster deeper understanding. The system would be designed to incorporate operating principles of what is presently known about human cognition and learning.

The group discussed the roles computers could play. Participants really wanted students to be immersed in a multisensory way in how the world works, and the computer could play several roles. It could help extend students' explorations beyond what they could otherwise experience by offering them simulations to overcome size, time scale, and safety constraints. Teachers and students could have the experience of performing experiments that cannot be done in the physical world. The group thought that the system should incorporate both simulation and modeling tools.

There was some discussion about the definition of "immersion." Some questioned whether immersion had to be through technology. Most participants agreed that they wanted students to be immersed in the multisensory experiences, but that immersion would sometimes be through technology and sometimes through real-world materials.

The group wanted software to support interpretation of collected data. The members thought having multiple representations of the same data to compare and contrast would be helpful. They also wanted students to be able to explore the world around them, take measurements from it, and discover how it works. Therefore, probes and sensors should be available for real-time data collection.

Some participants raised the idea of incorporating digital networks to extend knowledge and resource bases for both teachers and students. By sharing data and collaborating with classrooms beyond their own, students could make a system more comprehensive and useful than any single component. Participants were also committed to including lifelong professional development, from preservice onward, for all levels of school personnel.

Finally, the group suggested that they did not have time to consider other important issues related to development of a learning environment for eighth-grade science. They did not talk about particular learning objectives (except for inquiry), how to use technology to address topics or concepts that students find difficult, or any particular software that could address these issues. They also did not concentrate on challenges that are unique to middle schoolers: For instance, what do they enjoy? What will engage them? The breakout session did not discuss classroom issues, but surmised that the next step would be to consider the alignment with the *National Science Education Standards* (NRC, 1996a) content for eighth grade.

The representatives from the IT community emphasized the need to have a vision of IT in the near future—both the power and low cost of technology—and they encouraged representatives of the other sectors not to be constrained by current realities. For example, storage media are becoming so compact that in five years a student will be able to carry all of his or her schoolwork on something as small as a diskette or smart card for a computer station. That means that the participants' focus on the Web may be too specific. Soon it may be possible to carry around enough data in one's pocket to make Web access much less important that it is now.

Although they were often visionary themselves, the educators in the group frequently reminded everyone of the realities they face in their classrooms. For example, teachers spend a great deal of time worrying about meeting the criteria, standards, and assessment systems imposed on them.

The facilitator commented that the learning sciences researchers, who had a foot in both worlds and were really cautious in some respects, constantly took a scientific perspective as they considered how to incorporate the sciences of learning into the practice of teaching.

At the end of this session, each person made a statement about the breakout activity. The facilitator believed that everyone thought that if the group had really wanted to move to the specific design process as an exercise, it would have been helpful to have a more detailed problem. Yet this lack of a specified problem did not prevent them from discussing many issues, and she commented that she suspected anyone considering a design problem would do a lot of that work up front, talking about the constraints, assumptions, and design issues in order to understand the problem, just as this group did.

Finally, group members were unanimous in agreeing that they did not want technology to be the center of everything. They wanted technology to aid in the teaching and learning of science, but not to be either the primary objective or the primary focus.

3

Continuing the Conversation

At the conclusion of the symposium, many participants thought that there was a real opportunity to foster improved learning via information technology. Technology has become cheaper, more powerful, and more nearly ubiquitous. Concurrently, knowledge about how people learn is much richer. And there is a national resolve to find ways to improve K-12 education. The ILIT committee can maximize this opportunity by building a community of people from the three constituencies who can become adept at working closely together.

THE ILIT COMMITTEE'S CHARGE TO THE NATION

Rapid technological advances and breakthrough research in the learning and cognitive sciences, combined with a national commitment to improve learning, have finally provided the opportunity for true cross-fertilization of ideas for improving teaching and learning through the enlightened use of information technology. Rarely have these three stakeholder communities come together to grapple seriously with how to harness the power of information technology for use in the K-12 public education system. It is the ILIT committee's hope, and its charge to these communities, that they will work together in close collaboration because only such a coordinated effort can offer the best chance for fundamentally rethinking and transforming education in the United States.

The National Academies invites others with expertise in information technology and computer sciences, the cognitive and learning sciences, and the practice of education to contribute to this educational revolution by guiding the committee in its further deliberations. The National Research Council's Center for Education (CFE) has established a website, <http://www.nrcilit.org>, and will host workshops across the country to continue building a common vocabulary and a vision enriched by the wisdom and experience of these three vital, yet currently unconnected, communities. Interested individuals and stakeholders are encouraged to visit the website, participate in one of the meetings, and contact committee members and CFE staff to offer additional ideas about how to achieve the ILIT project goals.

NEXT STEPS

Participants were urged to discuss ways to continue the progress made during the meeting. The following ideas were offered:

- **Website.** Constructing a website was considered a priority. A website would enable interested parties, symposia attendees, and others to participate. It could serve to recap activities, post important papers, and link to useful URLs and other materials that these emerging allies might find interesting. For instance, an earlier National Academies project, the Impact of Information Technology on the Future of the Research University, resulted in a professionally videotaped and edited program of four two-hour segments that were broadcast on the ResearchChannel.[1] While the target audience was not large, this is one example of a method the ILIT project could use to build the communities' common vocabulary and catalyze collaborative partnerships.
- **Emerging Technologies.** One participant, recognizing a need for a better grasp on emerging technologies, thought a future meeting or workshop should include a demonstration of the emerging technologies to

---

[1]The ResearchChannel (formerly ResearchTV) was founded by a core group of research universities and corporate research divisions dedicated to broadening the access to and appreciation of the individual and collective activities, ideas, and opportunities in basic and applied research. One of the major goals of the ResearchChannel is to use content, content creation, and manipulation processes as a workbench to test materials for future analog and digital broadcast and on-demand multimedia offerings, thus providing an unusual opportunity to experiment with new methods of distribution and interaction on a global basis. More information on the ResearchChannel is available at <http://www.researchchannel.com>.

prompt a fruitful discussion of far-reaching visions. She felt the group still lacked a concrete sense of where technology is headed.

- **Leadership Institute.** Based on his experience, one participant stated that a leadership institute meeting would be useful. It would have to be designed very carefully, but he thought this model could work well in fostering dialogue with leaders and decision makers.
- **National Commission or National Summit.** Educational policy is enacted at the state level. A participant suggested that some of the ideas generated at the symposium could inform a national commission or a national summit convened by governors. This summit would provide the state education leaders with background information, data, and a structure. The commission could develop a plan to help the ILIT committee scale up, using the state education communities' pertinent experiences. After the commission had completed its work, which would have a finite period, there would be a follow-up activity. He envisioned that this would be a 10-year plan with different phases. He challenged the participants to think on a grand scale if they were serious about a long-term commitment to the goals of the ILIT project.

Another participant countered that some states, such as California and Texas, are so big that the state education commission is a small entity. Cities like New York City and Los Angeles, which educate large percentages of the nation's students, do not consider themselves part of any other governmental entity. She also mentioned that some university systems, such as the University of California and the California State University, consider themselves independent of their states; in fact, the University of California is constitutionally separate from the state government and independent in its governance and planning. This means that designers of any national plan to improve teaching and learning with IT need to fashion multiple strategies. They need to consider disparate spheres of influence, the variety of influences affecting these spheres, and the different ways that information flows.

- **Partners.** One symposium attendee thought that partnering with the Education Commission of the States (ECS) on a mutual effort would be productive. ECS is a bipartisan commission that is directed by a governor and includes state legislators who often control what happens in education.

Another participant commented that there already are a number of case studies that exemplify coordination of the different communities, but they are community based rather than professional-society based. And yet each of the sectors represented at this symposium has one or more professional societies, the goals of which are to provide leadership and cohesion (e.g., the Software & Information Industry Association, National School Board Association, Council of Chief State School Officers, and TechNet). He suggested that the ILIT committee discover how best to work with these organizations. He concluded that there was probably a short list of groups that could offer policy leverage points for addressing the many issues identified during the symposium.

To follow up on this issue, one participant commented that he was worried about the current disconnect between political and popular pressures to solve what is perceived as the "education problem." He asked whether the National Academies could construct a briefing team to be available to speak to various groups. Wulf responded that the National Academies often will convene a group of people to brief congressional staffers, agency personnel, and other interested parties about its reports. However, the National Academies must be extremely careful never to become advocates, or to be perceived as such, because they would lose their special credibility. Nevertheless, he did think briefings at professional society meetings on these issues are possible.

One participant recalled that the National Academies had convened representatives from "smoke-stack industries" several years ago to meet Academy members and discuss science, technology, and economic policy. She suggested that it might be worthwhile for the Academies to revive this practice and include representatives of the high-tech industry. She recommended some kind of mechanism to convene a meeting for the purpose of talking with leading scientists who can challenge conventional thinking.

- **Additional Meetings/Symposia.** Many participants were eager to continue the conversation through these "face-to-face" meetings. As Wulf admitted, even he felt that technology cannot yet make people who live in different places and do not know each other personally feel that they are part of a community. But he also hoped that the Web discussion site would facilitate continuing the conversation.

One participant suggested that if the National Academies sponsors further convocations, they should build on previous work. For instance, another meeting could concentrate on current technology and how to use it in ways that are unfamiliar to teachers. Another meeting could address tracking more of what students know and do.

She reminded the other participants that all education is local. Nationally aware and attuned groups like those at this symposium tend to think and speak in general terms and to attract "the usual suspects." She thought the ILIT committee should use the results of its conversation and community-building efforts to conduct state-oriented meetings.

Another participant added that the goal would be to interconnect all these strategies. For example, the local meetings could be advertised ahead of time with radio interviews and other outreach activities, and they could then be supported on the website with continuing discussions.

- **Emphasizing Education Supported by Technology Versus Skills Acquisition.** One participant offered a corollary point to the above suggestion. He commented that it was refreshing at this meeting to focus exclusively on education supported by technology. But in many communities, the educational focus in K-12 technology is almost entirely on skills acquisition. Industry and even state representatives talk about the skills gap, which translates into students' ability to use the Office tool suite and related applications. Technology in science is equated with the ability to compose PowerPoint presentations or to program in Visual Basic. He encouraged continued efforts to focus on how technology can transform teaching and learning in positive ways.

- **The Changing Nature of Knowledge.** One participant noted that the *National Science Education Standards* exist as one way of encouraging the changing nature of knowledge, but he commented that if people start thinking seriously about incorporating technology in all aspects of education, the *Standards* will have to evolve. This speaker, a professor, administrator, and technologist, thought it would be natural for the National Academies to undertake any revision process, particularly if the practices of science and engineering and the roles of mathematics in science and engineering are evolving. The National Academies can convey the idea that the technologies are part of the change methodology of the profession. This, in turn, would elevate the public discourse about what science and mathematics education is.

- **Keep It Simple Initially.** One participant remarked that he thought there was a huge amount of educational improvement to be made without relying on killer applications or "rocket science." This comment aligns with the prevailing sentiment that the nation needs to make progress fairly rapidly in education. He offered the following example to illustrate his point: The state government of Washington has done a good job of putting electronic services online. Each state agency wanted to use 10 percent of the applications that affect 90 percent of the work (as opposed to 90 percent of the applications that affect only 10 percent of the work).

Discipline was imposed in getting state agencies to focus on electronic services that actually touched large numbers of citizens without relying on cutting-edge advances (and their inherent costliness). That could happen in the educational domain as well.

- **Increased Accountability.** A principal from a large urban school district reminded the participants of the country's increased demand for accountability. She commented that there were some important things to keep in mind under the current political agenda with calls for accountability and improving test scores: How can stakeholders convert that data collection into a strategy that enables educators, learning scientists, and technologists to show how IT is making crucial differences to teaching and learning? How can technology's power for data collection be turned into an answer to critics seeking documentable proof about the efficacy of technology in improving education?

- **A Megaversity.** One participant commented that, in California, there has been an emerging effort to wire all nonprofits and educational institutions to foster a kind of "megaversity." He thought that NAS member Larry Smarr at the University of California, San Diego was a driving force behind this effort. He suggested that ILIT members contact him for his view of this issue.

- **Online Journal.** One participant suggested building an online journal from the grassroots up. This journal would include both pedagogical and content articles of interest to all the relevant communities.

- **Meta-reflection on the ILIT Challenge.** One participant commented that he had heard two processes being discussed at the symposium. The first concerned the convergence of social challenges and opportunities, technological challenges and opportunities, and new knowledge about how we learn. The question before the participants was what to do about that convergence and that opportunity. In the course of the discussions, participants learned that a lot is already being done. One process goal, therefore, is to augment specific successful exemplars—automating their functions and making the systems faster, better, and cheaper, thereby generating greater distribution and greater use. This strategy would encourage incremental successes or progress along a trajectory toward the bigger goal.

The other process is the challenge to move toward a more profound vision—that is, a deeper understanding of how to do new things in new ways with new processes. Participants also considered the need for better understanding of assessment or progress and the science and art of implementing strategies in a complex, multidisciplinary environment within the vagaries of political winds. Building further on this idea, another participant mentioned that there are different time lines of change in the systems that the groups discussed. Technology is changing very rapidly. Students are adapting quickly to a fast-paced world, thanks in large measure to the influence of the entertainment industry. Teachers are changing more slowly, schools more slowly yet. On what time line is implementation expected?

- **Concluding Remarks.** One participant concluded that he had rarely come to a conference where he was able to see that the whole is truly greater than the sum of its parts. The symposium proposed the question: Is there value in community among these three isolated groups? For many participants, the answer was an emphatic "yes." The collective efforts to address the design problems proved this to him. He encouraged the National Academies to build on this momentum.

SOLICITATIONS AND REQUESTS

This final conversation also netted concrete needs to continue the work begun at this symposium.

- **Solicitation for Funding Partners.** Wulf solicited suggestions of potential funding partners to sponsor additional symposia.
- **Solicitation for Local Symposium Hosts.** Wulf challenged participants to consider asking their communities to sponsor a local version of this national symposium.
- **Solicitation for References.** ILIT staff requested links to important documents and relevant organizations to share what ILIT is doing and to construct alliances. One participant commented that the National Academy of Education was undertaking a project on teacher education and should be contacted. Another mentioned that the North Central Regional Educational Lab was hosting a national panel and conference on emerging technologies in education.

Another person suggested linking to some of the research reports, such as the recent E-Learning report; the online report of the Congressional Commission on Web-based Education, which held regional hearings on this issue; and the fourth stage of the report for the CEO Forum on Education and Technology. She stated that these key reports support much of the ILIT symposium discussion and also provide a forward direction.

References

Carvin, A. (2000). (Ed.). *The E-rate in America: A tale of four cities.* Benton Foundation Communications Policy and Practice Program. Washington, DC: Author. Available: <http://www.benton.org/e-rate/e-rate.4cities.pdf> [3/5/02].

Cattagni, A., and Ferris, E. (2001). *Internet access in U.S. public schools and classrooms: 1994-2000* (NCES 2001–071). U.S. Department of Education, National Center for Education Statistics. Washington, DC: U.S. Government Printing Office. Available: <http://nces.ed.gov/pubs2001/2001071.pdf> [1/28/02].

CEO Forum on Education and Technology. (1999). *Professional development: A link to better learning. The CEO Forum school technology and readiness report-year two.* Washington, DC: Author.

CEO Forum on Education and Technology. (2000). *Teacher preparation staR chart: A self-assessment tool for colleges of education - preparing a new generation of teachers.* Washington, DC: Author.

Cuban, L. (2001). *Oversold and underused: Computers in the classroom.* Cambridge, MA: Harvard University Press.

Darling-Hammond, L. (1996). *What matters most: Teaching for America's future.* Kutztown, PA: National Commission on Teaching and America's Future.

Darling-Hammond, L. (1997). *Doing what matters most: Investing in quality teaching.* Kutztown, PA: National Commission on Teaching and America's Future.

Friedman, T. (1999). Next, it's E-ducation. *New York Times*, A29, November 17.

Gilder, G. (1993). Metcalfe's law and legacy. *Forbes ASAP 152*: Supplement (September 13), 158-166.

Hussar, W. J. (1999). *Predicting the need for newly hired teachers in the United States* (NCES 1999-026). Washington, DC: U.S. Government Printing Office.

Kaput, J., and Roschelle, J. (1998). The mathematics of change and variation from a millennial perspective: New content, new context. In C. Hoyles, C. Morgan, and G. Woodhouse (Eds.), *Rethinking the mathematics curriculum.* London: Falmer Press.

Marshall, R., and Tucker, M. (1992). *Thinking for a living: Education and the wealth of nations.* New York: Basic Books.

Moe, M.T., Blodget, H., Armstrong, M.E., Bailey, K., Godsey, N., Smith, C., Thompson, T., and Wilson, S. (2000). *The knowledge web (Part 1: People power - fuel for the new economy).* New York: Merrill Lynch.

National Commission on Mathematics and Science Teaching for the 21st Century. (2000). *Before it's too late.* Jessup, MD: Education Publications Center.

National Research Council. (1996a). *National science education standards.* National Committee on Science Education Standards and Assessment. Center for Science, Mathematics, and Engineering Education. Washington, DC: National Academy Press. Available: <http://www.nap.edu/catalog/4962.html> [1/28/02].

National Research Council. (1996b). *The preparation of teachers of mathematics: Considerations and challenges. A letter report.* Mathematical Sciences Education Board, Center for Science, Mathematics, and Engineering Education. Washington, DC: National Academy Press. Available: <http://www.nap.edu/catalog/10055.html> [1/28/02].

National Research Council. (1997). *More than screen deep: Toward every-citizen interfaces to the nation's information infrastructure.* Computer Science and Telecommunications Board. Washington, DC: National Academy Press. Available: <http://www.nap.edu/catalog/5780.html> [1/28/02].

National Research Council. (1998). *High stakes: Testing for tracking, promotion, and graduation.* Committee on Appropriate Test Use, J. Heubert and R. Hauser (Eds.). Division of Behavioral and Social Sciences and Education. Washington, DC: National Academy Press. Available: <http://www.nap.edu/catalog/6336.html> [1/28/02]

National Research Council. (1999a). *Being fluent with information technology.* Computer Science and Telecommunications Board. Washington, DC: National Academy Press. Available: <http://www.nap.edu/catalog/6482.html> [1/28/02].

National Research Council. (1999b). *How people learn: Brain, mind, experience, and school.* Committee on Developments in the Science of Learning, J. Bransford, A. Brown, and R. Cocking (Eds.). Division of Behavioral and Social Sciences and Education. Washington, DC: National Academy Press. Available: <http://www.nap.edu/catalog/6160.html> [1/28/02].

National Research Council. (1999c). *How people learn: Bridging research and practice.* Committee on Learning Research and Educational Practice, M. Donovan, J. Bransford, and J. Pellegrino (Eds.). Division of Behavioral and Social Sciences and Education. National Academy Press, Washington, DC. Available: <http://www.nap.edu/catalog/9457.html> [1/28/02].

National Research Council. (1999d). *Transforming undergraduate education in science, mathematics, engineering, and technology.* Committee on Undergraduate Science Education. Center for Science, Mathematics, and Engineering Education. National Academy Press, Washington, DC. Available: <http://www.nap.edu/catalog/6453.html> [1/28/02].

National Research Council. (2000). *Educating teachers of science, mathematics, and technology: New practices for the new millennium.* Committee on Science and Mathematics Teacher Preparation. Center for Science, Mathematics, and Engineering Education.

Washington, DC: National Academy Press. Available: <http://www.nap.edu/catalog/9832.html> [1/28/02].
National Research Council. (2001). *Building a workforce for the information economy.* Committee on Workforce Needs in Information Technology. Board on Testing and Assessment; Board on Science, Technology, and Economic Policy; Office of Scientific and Engineering Personnel. Computer Science and Telecommunications Board. Washington, DC: National Academy Press. Available: <http://www.nap.edu/catalog/9830.html> [1/28/02].
National Telecommunications and Information Administration. (2000). *Falling through the net: Toward digital inclusion.* Washington, DC: U.S. Government Printing Office.
Olson, L. (2000). *Finding and keeping competent teachers.* Education Week Online. <http://www.edweek.org/sreports/qc00/templates/article.cfm?slug=intro.htm> [3/5/02].
Pea, R.D. (2001). Technology, equity, and K-12 learning. In R. Noll (Ed.), *Bridging the digital divide: California public affairs forum* (pp. 39-51). Sacramento, CA: California Council of Science and Technology.
President's Committee of Advisors on Science and Technology, Panel of Educational Technology. (1997). *Report to the President on the use of technology to strengthen K-12 education in the United States.* Washington, DC: U.S. Government Printing Office.
President's Information Technology Advisory Committee. (1999). *Information technology research: Investing in our future.* Arlington, VA: National Coordination Office for Computing, Information, and Communication. Available: <http://www.ccic.gov/ac/report/> [1/28/02].
Repenning, A., Ioannidou, A., and Zola, J. (2000). AgentSheets: End-user programmable simulation. *Journal of Artificial Societies and Social Simulation, 3*(3). Available: <http://www.soc.surrey.ac.uk/JASSS/3/3/forum/1.html> [1/28/02].
Sarnoff Labs. (2000). *The fourth wave of the Internet.* Presentation by Norman Winarsy at SRI International, Menlo Park, CA.
Shulman, L.S. (1987). Knowledge and teaching foundations of the new reform. *Harvard Education Review, 57,*1-22.
Stodolsky, S. (1988). *The subject matters: Classroom activity in math and social studies.* Chicago: University of Chicago Press.
Stokes, D.E. (1997). *Pasteur's quadrant: Basic science and technological innovation.* Washington, DC: Brookings Institution Press.
Web-Based Education Commission. (2000). *The power of the Internet for learning.* Washington, DC: U.S. Government Printing Office. Available: <http://www.ed.gov/offices/AC/WBEC/FinalReport/> [1/28/02].
Witten, I., and Frank, E. (2000). *Data mining.* San Francisco, CA: Morgan Kaufman.

Appendix A

Symposium Participant List

Marilyn Adams
BBN Technologies
Cambridge, MA

Rick Adrion
CISE/EIA
National Science Foundation
Arlington, VA

Barbara Allen
Project LemonLINK
Lemon Grove, CA

Geri Anderson-Nielson
Georgetown Day School
Washington, DC

Dan Atkins
Alliance for Community
    Technology
University of Michigan
Ann Arbor, MI

Marianne Bakia
Federation of American Scientists
Washington, DC

Clarence Bakken
Gunn High School
Palo Alto, CA

Lynne Bell
CISE–Science Education
University of Virginia
Charlottesville, VA

Randy Bell
CISE–Science Education
University of Virginia
Charlottesville, VA

John Benson
Evanston Township High School
Evanston, IL

John Bransford
Vanderbilt University
Nashville, TN

John Brecht
Digital Earth Project
SRI International
Menlo Park, CA

David Byer
Office of Postsecondary Education
U.S. Dept. of Education
Washington, DC

Terence Cannings
Department of Education
Pepperdine University
Culver City, CA

Fred Carrigg
Academic Programs
Union City School District
Union City, NJ

Linda Chaput
President & CEO
Cogito Learning Media
San Francisco, CA

Linda Charles
Classroom Connect
Brisbane, CA

Bob Colwell
Intel Corp.
Hillsboro, OR

Irene DaMota
Roberto Clemente High School
Chicago, IL

Dorothy Dart
Genetic Science Learning Center
University of Utah
Salt Lake City, Utah

Sharon Derry
Dept. of Educational Psychology
University of Wisconsin, Madison
Madison, WI

David Dwyer
Director of Education
    Technologies
Apple Computer, Inc.
Palo Alto, CA

Daniel Edelson
Department of Education & Social
    Policy
Northwestern University
Evanston, IL

Carol Edwards
Foundation for the Improvement
    of Education
National Education Association
Washington, DC

Ira Fishman
Mindsurf Networks
McLean, VA

Kathleen Fulton
Web-Based Education
　Commission
U.S. Dept. of Education
Washington, DC

Louis Gomez
School of Education & Social
　Policy
Northwestern University
Evanston, IL

Lavona Grow
Preparing Tomorrow's Teachers to
　Use Technology (PT3)
U.S. Dept. of Education
Washington, DC

Idit Harel
MaMaMedia
New York, NY

Hoyet Hemphill
NCREL
Naperville, IL

Andres Henriquez
EDC/Center for Children and
　Technology
New York, NY

Richard Hershman
National Education Knowledge
　Industry Association
Washington, DC

Tom Hinojosa
Center for Technology in Learning
SRI International
Menlo Park, CA

Randy Hinrichs
Microsoft Research Lab
Redmond, WA

Susan Hoban
University of Maryland Baltimore
　County and
NASA Goddard Space Flight
　Center
Greenbelt, MD

Donald Hyatt
Thomas Jefferson High School of
　Science and Technology
Alexandria, VA

Erik Jakobsson
Molecular and Integrative
　Physiology
University of Illinois
Urbana, IL

James Kaput
University of Massachusetts at
　Dartmouth
North Dartmouth, MA

Ken Kay
CSPP
Washington, DC

John G. Keating
Department of Computer Science
National University of Ireland,
  Maynooth
Maynooth, County Kildare,
  Ireland

Henry Kelly
Federation of American Scientists
Washington, DC

Kenneth Koedinger
Human-Computer Interaction
  Institute
Carnegie Mellon University
Pittsburgh, PA

Janet Kolodner
College of Computing
Georgia Institute of Technology
Atlanta, GA

Keith Krueger
Consortium for School
  Networking
Washington, DC

Darryl LaGace
Project LemonLINK
Lemon Grove, CA

Tom Landauer
Institute of Cognitive Science
University of Colorado
Boulder, CO

Edward D. Lazowska
Department of Computer Science
  and Engineering
University of Washington
Seattle, WA

Peter Lyman
School of Information
  Management & Systems
University of California, Berkeley
Berkeley, CA

Miriam Masullo
IBM Thomas J. Watson Research
  Center
Yorktown Heights, NY

Florence McGinn
Hunterdon Central Regional High
  School
Flemington, NJ

Barbara E. McMullen
Marist College
Poughkeepsie, NY

Bakhtiar Mikhak
Media Laboratory
Massachusetts Institute of
  Technology
Cambridge, MA

John D. Miller
Intel Architectural Labs
Intel
Hillsboro, OR

APPENDIX A 63

Penny Noyce
The Noyce Foundation
Weston, MA

Barbara O'Keefe
Speech Communication Studies
Northwestern University
Evanston, IL

Roy Pea (**Cochair**)
Stanford University
Stanford, CA

Randall E. Raymond
Dept. of Strategic Planning &
    Resource Analysis
Detroit Public Schools
Detroit, MI

Alexander Repenning
Department of Computer Science
University of Colorado, Boulder
Boulder, CO

Paul Reynolds
Computer Science Department
University of Virginia
Charlottesville, VA

Steven Ritter
Carnegie Learning
Pittsburgh, PA

Steven D. Rizzi
Advanced Information Technology
    Center
Annapolis, MD

Linda Roberts
Darnestown, MD

Jeff Rodamar
Planning and Evaluation Service
U.S. Dept. of Education
Washington, DC

Katherine G. Rodi
CEO Forum on Education and
    Technology
Infotech Strategies
Washington, DC

Jeremy Roschelle
Educational Software Components
    of Tomorrow
SRI International
Menlo Park, CA

Nora Sabelli
Department of Curriculum &
    Instruction
University of Texas at Austin
Austin, TX

Mark Schneiderman
Software & Information Industry
    Association
Washington, DC

Arthur D. Sheekey
State Leadership Center
Council of Chief State School
    Officers
Washington, DC

David Sibbet
The Grove Consultants
   International
San Francisco, CA

Gary P. Smith
Montgomery County Public
   Schools
Rockville, MD

Elizabeth Stage
University of California System
Sacramento, CA

Clara Tolbert
Texas Instruments
Hopewell, VA

Antoinette Torres
NACME
New York, NY

Uri Treisman
Charles A. Dana Center for Math
   & Science Education
University of Texas at Austin
Austin, TX

Linda Tsantis
Technology for Educators
Johns Hopkins University
Columbia, MD

David Vogt
Brainium.com
Vancouver, BC, Canada

Barbara Watkins
James McCosh Elementary School
Chicago, IL

Gabrielle Wienhausen
University of California, San Diego
La Jolla, CA

Wm. A. Wulf (**Cochair**)
National Academy of Engineering
Washington, DC

Elise Yoder
Carnegie Learning
Pittsburgh, PA

Lee Zia
HER/DUE
National Science Foundation
Arlington, VA

Appendix B

Symposium Agenda

National Academy of Sciences Building
2100 C St. NW
Washington, DC

Wednesday, January 24, 2001

NAS AUDITORIUM

8:30 am	Welcome and Overview, Wm. A. Wulf & Roy Pea
9:00 am	Opening Remarks, Linda Roberts
9:30 am	Exercise to Build a Common Language, David Sibbet
10:15 am	Break
10:30 am	Building a Common Language (cont.)
Noon	Lunch
1:00 pm	Breakout Groups on Successful Partnerships

                Case 1: Project LemonLINK, Barbara Allen, Darryl LaGace
                NAS 150 – Facilitator, Kathleen Fulton

                Case 2: Union City Public Schools, Fred Carrigg, Steven Perez, José Marrero
                NAS 180 – Facilitator, David Dwyer

Case 3: Chicago City Science Program, Barbara Watkins, Irene DaMota, Louis Gomez
NAS 280 – Facilitator, Dan Atkins

Case 4: SimCalc Project, James Kaput
Lecture Room – Facilitator, David Sibbet

3:00 pm   Break

3:30 pm   Reports from Breakout Groups

GREAT HALL
4:30 pm   Technology Demonstrations
(open until the end of the reception)

Classroom Connect
AgentSheets
Teachscape
Cognitive Tutors for Mathematics
Educational Software Components of Tomorrow
WorldWatcher
Digital Earth Follow-on Project
SimCalc

5:00 pm   Reception

NAS AUDITORIUM
5:45 pm   Welcome, Wm. A. Wulf & Roy Pea

6:00 pm   *How People Learn*, John Bransford

6:45 pm   Talk on K-12 Education Issues, Nora Sabelli

7:30 pm   Closing Remarks, Wm. A. Wulf & Roy Pea

GREAT HALL
8:15 pm   Dinner

9:30 pm   Adjourn

APPENDIX B 67

Thursday, January 25, 2001

NAS LECTURE ROOM

8:30 am Overview of the Day's Agenda Wm. A. Wulf & Roy Pea

8:45 am Learning to Work Together: Breakout Groups Around Three Design Scenarios Using Information Technology

    Scenario 1: Creating an Advanced Placement Calculus Course for a Rural High School
    NAS 180 – Facilitators, Jeremy Roschelle & Uri Treisman

    Scenario 2: Enhancing Literacy in Children: Reading to Learn
    NAS 250 – Facilitators, Marilyn Adams & Tom Landauer

    Scenario 3a: Developing Environments for Learning Eighth Grade Science
    NAS Auditorium – Facilitator, Elizabeth Stage

    Scenario 3b: Developing Environments for Learning Eighth Grade Science
    Lecture Room – Facilitator, Sharon Derry

10:15 am Break

10:30 am Breakout Groups (cont.)

Noon Working Lunch—Reports from the Breakout Groups

1:30 pm Reflections on the Workshop

2:45 pm Closing remarks, Wm. A. Wulf & Roy Pea

3:00 pm Adjourn